My Dizney, Kentucky Appalachian Mountain Ancestors

My Dizney, Kentucky Appalachian Mountain Ancestors

Portia Cloud-Banach

iUniverse, Inc.
New York Lincoln Shanghai

My Dizney, Kentucky Appalachian Mountain Ancestors

iUniverse books may be ordered through booksellers or by contacting:

iUniverse
2021 Pine Lake Road, Suite 100
Lincoln, NE 68512
www.iuniverse.com
1-800-Authors (1-800-288-4677)

Because of the dynamic nature of the Internet, any Web addresses or links contained in this book may have changed since publication and may no longer be valid.

The views expressed in this work are solely those of the author and do not necessarily reflect the views of the publisher, and the publisher hereby disclaims any responsibility for them.

ISBN: 978-0-595-46480-7 (pbk)
ISBN: 978-0-595-90779-3 (ebk)

Printed in the United States of America

In the middle 1990s I decided to start writing down the memories of my childhood to preserve the history of a little Appalachian town of Dizney, Kentucky. I did not want these memories to be lost to my nieces, cousins, children and grandchildren.

So I began my journey back in time. This was very therapeutic for me. I was able to deal with many hang-ups about growing up in poverty with polio in the 1950s.

I am relying on the memories of myself and other family members for the stories in this book. I do not presume to say that every word in this book is a fact. Some of the information I obtained from State archives such as marriage records, death records, cemetery records, legal records and the internet. I am not a professional genealogist.

I met quite a few cousins on the internet that I never knew about. I re-connected with a few people from Dizney who had moved away. The internet was a wealth of information. There are thousands of sites that are dedicated to genealogy. I found a few family trees dealing with the Cloud family history. A lot of people were very willing to help me out. I have found three or four family trees of the Cloud family on the internet. The Cloud Association did a fine job tracing the Cloud family back to the 1500s in England. But none of them match the records my father gave me. So I elected to start my search from the information my family had already.

Trying to figure out who was right was impossible so I began my own quest for as much of the truth as possible. My father gave me a written history of his grandfather Benjamin Franklin Cloud, which was written by one of his father's sisters children. These cousins also gave my dad a written history and family tree of the William Henry Shoemaker family. These were the oral memories of their mother. Daddy also gave me a written list of his mother's family, Andrew Jackson and Drucilla Hall Presley and their children. Dad did not say where he got this list. My dad was very much interested in preserving his family's history.

My mother and father told me stories of how they grew up in the mountains of Harlan County, Kentucky. My father told stories of his grandfather and his brothers once I showed an interest in our families past.

Family members have generously given me copies of pictures. Friends have shared pictures that have been handed down to them by their family.

I appreciate and thank all those that helped me with my quest to gather as many stories and pictures as I could get to help with my web page.

In the middle 1990s I decided to try and make a web site for the pictures and stories that I had written. The more I wrote the more I remembered.

This book is dedicated to my cousins Alene Presley Gilbert and Helen Presley Jones who inspired me with their family tree search. Alene gave me some wonderful pictures. Helen and her daughter Kim kept an eye out for documents and pictures that I would be interested in as they did their research. Alene and Helen passed away before I decided to write this book.

"To forget one's ancestors is to be a brook without a source, a tree without a root"

—Author unknown

Contents

Preface

I was born in 1948 in Dizney, Harlan County, Kentucky. My story is about my growing up in Stretchneck Holler, Dizney, Kentucky in the 1950s with Polio. I became ill with Polio when I was eleven months old in 1949.

My father and grandfather were born in Dizney, Kentucky. My ancestors came to Harlan County, Kentucky around 1800. Other ancestors came to Kentucky after the civil war. I began searching the internet genealogy sites for information on the history of my hometown and my ancestors in 1995. I did not want our family history to be lost to future generations. My nieces and nephews had no idea what it was like to grow up in the poverty of the coal mining towns of Eastern Kentucky.

My father gave me written information regarding some of our ancestors. I was given documents, stories and pictures from cousins and family members. Most of the stories in this book are the memories of my immediate family and friends.

My memories cover the period of the 1950s. We moved to Louisville, Kentucky in 1960.

1

The Pioneers of Harlan County, Kentucky

The first state representative from Harlan County, Kentucky was George Brittain. He is my 5th great grandfather. The Brittains were traced to the 1400s in Wales. There was an Earl in the Brittains line. The Cloud line was traced to the 1500s in England.

Leona Presley Cloud's father was half Cherokee Indian. His name was Andrew Jackson Presley. His family came to Harlan County, Kentucky in the 1880s from Tennessee. We believe his grandmother came from Virginia. Lots of American Indians married white men to hide their Indian nationality so that they would not be forced to go West by the federal government. There were Cherokee Indians that lived in the mountains of Harlan County that intermarried with white settlers who came to this area of Kentucky.

My mother's father is named James Hale. Her mother is Rebecca Woods Hale. They both came from Campbell County, Tennessee. Rebecca Woods' father's family was traced back to the Revolutionary War in the 1700. Rebecca Woods Hale's mother was a Wilson and her line was traced back to Lady Mary Boleyn, sister of Ann Boleyn in England. All of my relatives have been in the United States since the 1700s.

The surnames from my father's family are Cloud, Middleton, Presley, Wynn, Bailey, Turner, Brennan, Hall and Chadwell. The ancestors from my mother's family are Hale, Woods, Wilson, Housley and Ousley.

The Hale family came from England. I would not be at all surprised if they are descendants of the original Nathan Hale family who immigrated

1

here before the war of independence with England. They were here for the revolutionary war. The Clouds came to America with William Penn. The first Cloud family settled in or near Philadelphia and in Delaware. They so admired Benjamin Franklin that it would become a tradition to name at least one son Benjamin Franklin Cloud.

Three generations before my great grandfather Benjamin Franklin Cloud were also named Benjamin Franklin Cloud. Many sons of those first emigrants went south to Maryland, Virginia, Tennessee, North Carolina, and west to Texas, and Missouri.

Benjamin Franklin Cloud III and Nancy Middleton were married in Claiborne County Tennessee in 1857 or 1858. Their fifth child, James was born in Harlan County, Kentucky. Ben Frank Cloud and Nancy lived on the Cloud Branch of the Yokum Creek holler on top of the mountain with their family. When their children got married and started their families they moved down the mountain a short distance from their parents.

From Evarts to Dizney was known as Yokum Creek. Yokum Creek had been established before the start of the civil war. Harlan County, Kentucky's first recorded wedding was 1818, only six short years after the war of 1812.

Some old family names in Dizney were Middleton, Cloud, Jones, Singo, Pace, Madden, Turner, Wynn, Thomas, Cox, Brewer, Blevins and Presley. Most of the earlier settlers came to Dizney from Tennessee and Virginia.

Elijah Frank Dizney was the head instructor at the Presbyterian Black Mountain Academy which had been built in Evarts, Kentucky and was the predecessor of Evarts High School. Dizney, Kentucky was probably named after Elijah Dizney. The next school known as Black Mountain Academy was headed by Elijah Dizney also. It was built in Black Mountain, just below Kenvir, on the mountain behind the Red Store.

The only way to reach those family homes in the beginning was by foot, horse, mule and wagon. Those old time settlers came down in the summer and late fall, after harvest time, to trade, barter and swap for the necessities to last them for the entire summer or winter. Spring was too busy planting crops and early fall was too busy harvesting to come down off the mountain. They were self-sustaining individuals. They made their own clothes, food, built their own log cabins, animal shelters and whatever else that was necessary to their way of life.

Junior Cloud (my father) told me of his visits to the top of the mountain in Yokum Creek to visit his great aunt Seripta, daughter of Ben Cloud and Nancy Middleton Cloud. He liked to visit his grandfather's brothers too.

He listened to stories of when they first moved to the hills of Kentucky. The kids would have to take off their shoes as soon as the last snow melted and not replace them until the snows fell again in the beginning of winter. This was to save on the wear and tear of their shoes. Everyone ran around barefoot. The only danger was that of being bitten by snakes and maybe stepping on a dead poisonous snake that still had poison in their fangs, which was just as deadly.

There were four hollers in Dizney. The families that lived in Bill's creek holler were Blevins, Cox, Brewer and Gilbert. The families that lived in Turner's creek holler were Thomas, Middleton, Singo and Wynn. The families who lived in Yokum creek holler were Cloud, Jones and Cornett. In Stretchneck holler the families were Cloud, and Presley. I am not sure why Stretchneck holler did not have the name creek to it like the other hollers did.

There were lots of families that moved to Harlan County in the early 1900s to work in the coal mines. My mother told me that there was a coal mine run by Garfield McLean in Reds Creek holler between Kenvir and Dizney where daddy worked after the mines in Kenvir and Black Mountain closed down. There were also mines that were just over the mountain in Virginia at the head of the mountain range that bordered with Virginia. The Virginia mines had track with a coal car that would be sent to the top of the mountain to pick up the Kentucky workers and take them down the mountain to the Virginia mine. This area was referred to as Bonnie Blue, Virginia.

Dizney was not a township, corporation or any type of formed government. There wasn't a police department, fire department or any organized body of citizens to keep law and order. In the late 1800s mail came by horseback rider. A post office was established for Dizney in the early 1900s when the coal mines were booming. The post office was moved to Black Mountain as it was the most thriving community after the 1920s when two mines opened in the Kenvir area.

The families that came to live in America brought their religious beliefs and values with them. These beliefs were influenced by the Quakers and other religious groups searching for religious freedom. Most of the people of the Appalachian mountain region of Kentucky, Virginia and Tennessee came from England, Scotland, Ireland and Wales. They ended up bringing much more. Their music, songs, story telling and culture still remain with the people of South Eastern Kentucky to this day.

Their beliefs were puritan in nature. The bible was taken as the one and only word of God. They apparently did not understand parables as Jesus preached. The women's form of dress was long sleeves, dresses down to the top of their shoes. They could not cut their hair. The puritanical morals were handed down from generation to generation even into the 20th Century.

The rules to live by were taught in the school and church. The only law was the 10 commandments and the golden rule. There was a small one room school in the late 1800s that set at the mouth of Stretchneck holler that also was the community church on Sunday. There was nothing like a good fire and brimstone sermon to make everyone, young and old, quiver in his boots or shoes and walk the straight and narrow path until next Sunday. Most people were honest as the day was long and would never dream of doing anything that Jesus and their mothers would be ashamed of.

Dizney was almost a mirror image of a Wild West town. My father (Junior Cloud) had heard stories from his grandma Presley about Jesse James visiting Dizney. This is possible, because my great grandfather Andrew Jackson Presley had a brother named Jesse James Presley. Guns and shotguns were carried by almost everyone, male and female. Pistols were for protection. You never knew when you would meet some dangerous human or rattlesnake in the woods surrounding Dizney.

Shotguns were for hunting rabbits, squirrels, fur pelts from foxes, beaver and minks. Also there were bears, wild cats, panthers and rabid animals to protect against.

There were feuds, bad blood between families that carried from one generation to the next. One of Ben's (Benjamin Franklin Cloud, Jr.) brothers death certificate reads that he was found floating face down in a stream with a bullet in his head, conclusion murder. I remember having the impression as a child that people named Napier were not liked by my father or his father. I did not understand until I started digging into our family history that a Napier from Dizney was responsible for getting people to give false testimony that sent Great grandpa Benjamin Cloud to prison.

Tilman Thomas Cloud was the first generation of the family to grow up in Dizney. He was born in 1901. He married Leona Presley in the middle 1920s. They lived in Brittans Creek until 1928 when they moved into a cabin at the head of Stretch Neck holler. Tilman Cloud eventually bought the house below this cabin and lived there the rest of his life.

Leona Presley Cloud was born in Dizney, Kentucky. I have school census from the early 1900s on Drucilla and Andrew Jackson Presley's children. Drucilla's descendants were established in Harlan County in the early 1800's. My Presley cousins have traced them to George Brennan who was a prominent legislator. The Chadwell family married into the Cloud family. The Clouds, Chadwells, and Brennans came together in the corner of Tennessee, Virginia and Kentucky during the revolutionary and war of 1812.

2

How Pumpkin Center got its name.
As told to Sue Jones by Minnie Presley Benge.

This is Sue Jones coming at you with the answer of Pumpkin Center. Don't mean to take my son Chris' place when it comes to history.

How "Punkin Center" got its same, according to Minnie (Presley) Benge. Minnie was born in 1910. Her parents were Jess Presley and Elizabeth Wynn Presley. Minnie is 97 years young.

Minnie has lived in Dizney, Kentucky most of her life. She had an Uncle by the name of Ben Wynn (a bachelor fellow). Ben was from Virginia. He worked in a coal mines in Virginia. The coal mines paid him in silver dollars. Ben Wynn would cross "Bonnie Blue" mountain above Punkin Center on his way to and from work.

He gave Minnie his silver dollars to keep for him. She kept them in an old coffee can. When Ben got enough silver dollars saved he went out and bought himself a phonograph. The old timers did enjoy their music. Minnie said it looked like a sewing machine.

Ben decided he wanted himself a record, so he goes and buys a record by Uncle Dave Mackon. This record looked like a tin can. The name of the song was "Punkin Center", wouldn't you know it. Uncle Ben Wynn liked this song so much he started calling Dizney "Punkin Center" So I guess the name stuck.

This is a true story as told by Minnie who still lives in Punkin Center in a little house next to the Baptist Church. Now you have the story of Punkin Center, Dizney, Ky.

Extra history! Uncle Ben finally came back to Dizney from Virginia and opened a small grocery store in what they call "Stretch Neck Holler. Ben Wynn is buried at Bill's Creek cemetery. I don't know how "Stretchneck Holler" got its name. Hope you enjoy this story. I told this exactly the way Minnie told it to me on October 28, 2002.

Minnie Presley Binge is the niece to Andrew Jackson and Drucilla Presley. Her parents were Elizabeth Wynn and Jess Presley. Elizabeth's sister, Mary Jane Wynn married Frank Cloud and lived most of her life in Stretch Neck Holler. Elizabeth and Mary Jane were sisters to Ackles Wynn who was at one time a pastor at the Dizney and Kenvir Baptist Churches.

3

Dizney, Kentucky

In the little town of Dizney, Kentucky in the 40s and 50's there were two general stores. The Pace family had a store and the Jones brothers had a store. There were two churches, Locust Grove Baptist Church and the Pentecostal Church of God. A public transportation bus ran every day from Harlan, Ky.

The post office at Dizney was first opened in 1896. In 1912 the post office was moved to Kenvir, Kentucky, which was about three miles away from Dizney, Kentucky. In 1922 another post office was opened in Dizney, Kentucky.

There was an important local trail used by area people in the early to late 1800s and early 1900s. This trail crosses over the mountain into Virginia from Dizney. The trail and mountain were referred to as "Bonnie Blue". Hundreds of people used to cross the mountain to do business and visit relatives in Virginia. The distance from Dizney to the Kentucky and Virginia line is only five miles.

There is an Indian burial ground on the top of Bonnie Blue Mountain, where old timers said Yocum Creek and Child's Creek head up together. There are Indian writings and pictures drawn in the mountains on rocks jutting out from the mountains.

My father, Junior Cloud told me a story that his grandma Drucilla Presley told him. They had a famous visitor at one time by the name of Jessie James. The tale must have been true because Grandpa Presley had a brother named Jesse James Presley.

The community revolved around the two churches. My family belonged to the Baptist Church. Every Sunday morning found my family at church, except for Dad. There would be songs, offerings and Sunday school classes would begin. The men would teach the classes for the boys and men and the women would teach the girls and women classes.

My favorite Sunday school teacher was Leona Cloud, my grandmother. She could make the people in the bible so real to us. I don't ever remember anyone whether teacher or preacher telling us to hate the Jews because they crucified Jesus. I never heard a prejudice word spoken against a black person or an Indian. There were some people in the early 1900s that were part Indian and part black. There was no separate town for black people in Dizney. The black children were raised by whatever family they were born into. We were pretty isolated in the hills of Southeastern Kentucky.

There were a few things that came as natural to some of the citizens in Dizney as going to church on Sunday. Those things were moonshine and home brew. The federal government spent many years trying to wipe out all the illegal stills in Harlan County, Kentucky. They never were able to wipe them out. There may not be any moonshiners left in Dizney anymore. In today's culture the most popular illegal substance is narcotics, prescription drugs and marijuana.

Guns were carried by most of the men and a few of the women. The men carried guns for protection, for killing wild game for food and killing snakes. My grandfather, Tilman Thomas Cloud's half sisters, Delilah and Nancy, carried guns in the pocket of their dresses. There were no law enforcement officers in this mountain town. There was a police station in Kenvir, Kentucky in the 1920s and 30s when the Peabody Coal Company started building the town for their workers. In the 1950 the only sheriff was the police who had an office in Evarts, which was 5 miles from Dizney. In the late 1960s I brought my future husband to visit my relatives in Dizney. He got a parking ticket while we were in Evarts. He told the story for years about his .25 cent parking ticket. He rolled the ticket around the quarter and pushed it under the door of the police station because there was no one there when we went to pay the ticket.

On July 4th there were not any fireworks or rockets shot into the sky, but the mountains would shake, rattle and roll after dark when daddy and his buddies would be chucking dynamite sticks from the top of the surrounding mountains. This was the best holiday of the year. Lots of relatives would come home for a visit and there would be lots of food and ice cream, with the celebrations. Most family reunions were held on this holiday.

I never really knew what Halloween was all about until I was 13 and moved to Louisville. Halloween did not mean much in my childhood, but mischief night sure did to the older kids. There were quite a few bad boys in Dizney. One mischief night after church service was over, we began walking up the road towards the big bridge at Stretchneck holler, and our flashlight spotted some very large boulders across the road. We had to wait for the men who were at church to move the boulders so that we could continue our walk home. The mischief makers would also overturn a select few outside toilets and others would be set on fire. Not very many people could afford costumes or candy for this holiday anyway.

There were a few bad boys that you just didn't want to mess with or to be caught out alone when you happened to encounter them. Two such boys lived in Stretchneck Holler. They were a source of torment for my brothers Roger and Tony. They would tease and intimidate. This was a surprise, as I think back on it, because most everyone in Dizney feared my dad. There were a couple of times that daddy left to work in Michigan. So it is possible daddy was not around and that was why the Ward boys were so brave. Daddy was constantly tormenting the kids with his teasing too.

Charles and Roby lived on the right side of the hill in Stretchneck Holler, across from Homer and Mary Ellen Cloud, just up the holler a little piece from my Aunt Pauline's house. Their house sat up on the hill but close enough to the dirt road to see who was coming and going in or out of Stretchneck Holler. Charles and Roby Ward had a really mean dog which they would sic on Roger and Tony.

One morning Roger and Tony were on their way out of the holler to catch the school bus. Just as they got close to the Ward boys house, out came their dog snarling and ready to eat them alive. Tony was scared to death but Roger had had enough of the Ward boys and their mean dog. When the dog got close enough Roger gave a kick to the dogs face. That sent the dog end over end down the road. I guess the dog figured out that pain was not much fun and he went whining home to sulk and never bothered Roger again.

Thanksgiving was a time for a solemn celebration. There would be a big dinner where thanks would be given to God for the blessings one had received. Even if the blessings were about the most basic of life's necessities, like having enough food to keep from starving, shoes to wear when it snowed, enough wood and coal to keep warm during the winter, the health of family and relatives.

There were a few shooting contests around Thanksgiving with the prize being a free turkey for the winner. Daddy was an excellent shot and would usually win a turkey. These shooting matches were a contest from the frontier settlers in the late 1700 and early 1800s. Keeping your shooting skills sharp would most likely save your life.

In December the participants in the Christmas play would start the weekly practice at the church. The play was always very inspirational and the choir sang beautifully. Most everyone attended the Christmas play, usually on the Saturday before Christmas.

On the Sunday before Christmas, everyone in Dizney would be at the church house for Sunday school and morning services. After services the children would line up, walk up to the front of the church where they would be handed a large paper bag with fruit, nuts, candy and gum. Then every adult would line up and receive their bag also. For many of the adults and children this would be the only time they would get such treats. I know that it was the only time that I received an orange each year. The only time I got to eat a peach was if a farmer happened to drive up to Dizney selling their fruit. There was never a shortage of apples or pears as they grew in the hills and valleys in Dizney.

In order to purchase groceries that the Jones store didn't carry you had to travel to the only supermarket close. That supermarket was named "Mack's" and was in the slightly bigger town of Evarts, Kentucky. Evarts was about five miles from Dizney.

The Dizney grade school building was in the shape of a U. The building faced the county road and was just past Yokum Creek Holler. Most of the children rode the school bus to school. The children in Bills Creek Holler and Stretchneck Holler walked to Milt Jones' store on the main road. Mom arranged for me to get picked up and let off at the "Big Bridge". The children from Turner's creek and Yokum creek walked to school.

The families that had husbands who worked in the coal mines and the ones who had no income got some form of Aid for Dependant children from the state. Mom would some how manage to get a ride into Evarts or Harlan to pick up the free food. We never owned a car when we lived in Dizney, Ky. The food she would bring home were peanut butter, rice, cheese, powdered milk, spam and some kind of canned hash with potatoes. The spam was used for breakfast when there was no pork left from the fall hog killing.

Bologna also tasted pretty good with eggs and biscuits. Jones store sold bologna and cheese and other sandwich meat. Daddy took spam sandwiches to work in the mines. He ate spam the rest of his life because he liked it a lot. We usually had a cow so mom probably gave the powered milk to other needy families. The cheese came in long square cardboard boxes. The cheese came in a long square shape that was sealed in plastic. Not much different than the cheese that you can buy sliced in supermarkets today.

A hospital was built by the Peabody Coal Company in Black Mountain, Kentucky. When the demand for coal dropped off the mines were closed and everything owned by the coal company closed down. The workers living in the coal camp houses were given a chance to buy the houses or were allowed to pay rent.

My father and grandfather, Junior and Tilman Cloud made their living working in the Peabody Coal Mines in camp #31 and #30. My father would come home with coal dust covering his entire body. Mom would have a wash tub full of warm water waiting for daddy's bath. Those filthy overalls, shirt and long johns must have been really hard to get clean on a scrub board. In the mid 50s daddy bought mom a wringer type washing machine.

Most every family had some kind of garden to grow food to feed their family. There were those who were too lazy to start a garden and they lived off handouts. My father had no use for anyone that was too lazy to feed and house their family. My mother had went hungry so often in her early childhood that she appreciated how hard daddy worked in his garden, maintaining his chickens and cows to feed us.

My brothers and I didn't get out of Stretchneck holler except to go to church or school. However in the summer if mom had to deliver something to a family who lived at the bottom of Stretchneck holler she would take us with her. My brothers would be allowed to play with the other children who lived in the valley at the beginning of Stretchneck Holler while mom and I visited who ever she had come down to see. We were not allowed to cross the bridge to the main road without mom.

So off mom and I would go to visit Eddie Mae Cloud who was the wife of Charlie Cloud, a cousin of my dads, or Grandma Presley or the Thomas family. I liked Eddie a lot and loved to hear her talk of old times. She had a young daughter Genevia who I admired. She was so pretty.

Sally Cloud, who could neither speak nor hear, was the wife of Cecil Cloud, a cousin of my dads. I loved Sally because her face was an open book and I could see the love for me in her eyes. She used sign language to speak. We grew up with Sally's children, Doris, Faye, Sargent and Mary Ellen. Cecil's brothers were Charlie, Will, Homer, Simon, Jess and Pearl Cloud. There were three sisters, Sarah, Rebecca and Emiline. These Cloud brothers and sisters were the grand children of Greenberry Cloud who was the brother of my great grandfather Benjamin Franklin Cloud.

The father and mother of these boys were Frank and Mary Jane Wynn Cloud. Frank and Mary Jane lived in a little house just past Homer and Mary Ellen's house. Their house sat on the right side of the creek, across a little foot bridge over the creek in a little flat area next to the mountain. They had a nice size property around their house compared to most of the people in Stretch Neck.

As a child Sheila and I would go to visit aunt Mary Jane and she would tell us ghost stories. Then we would have to get home before dark because we would be scared to death. Frank was the son of Greenberry and Clara Goodwin Cloud.

Rob and Jess Cloud lived below Pauline Grubbs, dad's sister. Rob and Pauline were great friends. The children that I remember of Jess and Rob were Shirley and Pauline "Little Pauline".

I loved going with mom to visit these families. I sat quietly and soaked up all the gossip and talk with the older folks. We visited the home of Pearl and Tildy who lived on the side of the mountain on the right side of the dirt road, above Home and Mary Ellen's house. There was a road just below Uncle Elmer Presley's house that ran around the side of the mountain to their house.

Stretchneck holler's families in the late 1940 and early 1950s were descendants of Greenberry Cloud's son Frank and all of his ten children, Benjamin Franklin Cloud's son Tilman and his son Junior and daughter Pauline and Grandma Presley's son Elmer Presley and his family.

4

A Look Back at the One Room School at Dizney By: Chris Jones

One room schools is a phrase that is synonymous with early rural education all over these United States. The Appalachian Mountains of East Kentucky in the early part of the 1900's had small one room schools in each little hamlet. In the case of Dizney the one room housed the school and the church.

The late Raymond Layne, who served in 1978 as the then editor of the "School Bell Echo" the official newsletter of the Madison County Retired Teachers Association, wrote an article on his early beginning as an educator in the hills of east Kentucky in a place on Yokums Creek in Harlan County, called Dizney.

Let us step back in time, as we again bring this article to light, showing how it was on Yokum Creek about 1922.

The spring term of school was rapidly coming to an end at Eastern Kentucky Normal School Now Eastern Kentucky University in Richmond Ky. As we were studying for exams, students were asking "Where will you be teaching this fall?" We didn't know because we still did not have a job.

President Coates announced that County school superintendents were coming to Eastern to interview graduating students as prospective teachers in their systems. We were very interested in being interviewed for a job.

The superintendent of Bracken County talked to us and then we went in to see Abner C. Jones, Superintendent of Harlan County Schools. Mr. Jones said he could use both of us, my wife and me. The salary was somewhat better than Bracken County was paying.

In due time, we got a letter saying we had been assigned to teach at Dizney, Kentucky. This school was at the head of Yocum Creek up from Evarts, Ky. We were given the name of the trustee and of the local merchant. We wrote to the storekeeper, Henry Surgener, who agreed to rent us two furnished rooms.

We had no money. We borrowed $100.00 from Berea Bank and Trust Co. to tide us over until we could make a "draw". We rode the train to Evarts were we made connections with the mail wagon. This was a farm jolt wagon pulled by two mules. We put our suit cases in the wagon with the packages and mail bag and headed up the creek. The rough rocky road followed along side the creek part of the way and IN the creek the rest of the way. Someone said we "forded" the creek lengthwise.

The Surgeners were friendly folks and we were soon settled in our two rooms. Henry gave us credit at the store for groceries and we did not have to pay rent until our check came in. We both taught in the same room, the Baptist Church, Locust Grove Missionary Baptist Church, which had leased by the county since the old log school housed had been condemned.

A revival was in progress when we arrived. We decided to wait a week for it to close before starting school. We kept busy by digging pits and erecting two "Outhouses" back of the Church house.

We no sooner had started school when three preachers came in and announced that they were starting another "protracted meeting". We were somewhat disgusted. This meant that every morning we would have to clean out the room of trash thrown on the floor by folks the night before. This sometimes filled a bushel basket.

Since this was our first time in the mountains of Harlan, we were a curiosity to the folks there and they were no less a curiosity to us. Many of the men we met on the road carried two 45 pistols or a rifle. We decided to stay in the house at night.

To make it easier to get the pupils in and out of the house we tool a portable phonograph to school and played marches for the children to walk in by. The next day, Bill Cloud, the trustee, came to school and ordered us to take that "Devil-Box" out of the Church house. He did not want no "Dancing" in the Church house.

We got a bubbler drinking fountain and set it on a table by the door. This was another "newfangled thing brung in from the lowlands" The trustee allowed we thought the kids were too nasty to drink after each other. They had always done it.

We erected swings and a merry-go-round and started supervised play on the yard. Many of the boys played marbles at recess time. Two fifth grade boys got to fussing over the game. I told them to stop or I would spank them. In a few minutes they were at it again. I picked up the Jones boy and spanked him soundly. Then I picked up the Pace boy to give him his punishment. He happened to have a penny box of kitchen matches in his hip pocket of his overalls. When I came down with my palm on him the matches ignited and literally burned a hole in his pants and blistered his hip. The word was soon spread over the community that Mr. Layne sot a boy on fire at school.

We stayed seven months in Dizney before coming to the flatlands. When we rolled into Richmond and got off the train, the land looked like it had been run over by a big roller and flattened out. We had spent very little of our money and had $1400.00 in the bank when we got home. I spent the next two years teaching in a coal camp on Wallins Creek. Our stay in Appalachia was very educational for us. We went back to Dizney 49 years later and could not even find the spot where we had lived. Things had changed so much we did not recognize places.

Note: The "Jones" boy who was spanked was my grandfather Milton Jones, I do not know who the Pace boy was. The Church was a one room clapboard frame structure which was torn down in 1947 to make room for the present building. Henry Surgener ran a country store and was postmaster at Dizney, before the business was sold and taken over by Arthur Pace. The new school building at Dizney was built on Turners creek to house the students, thus moving them from the church building. This building too is long gone. The students were consolidated with the Black Mountain School. The old Log school that had been condemned, sat near the mouth of Stretch-neck hollow, and was the first meeting site of the Locust Grove Baptist Church, which was established in 1885.

Thanks Chris for allowing me to put your story in my book.

5

The History of the Locust Grove Missionary Baptist Church of Dizney, Kentucky as told by Chris Jones.

The Locust Grove Missionary Baptist Church is situated on Highway #215 in Dizney Harlan County, Kentucky. The Church was established as a Missionary Baptist Church in the summer of 1885. William Henry Shoemaker, a Baptist pioneer preacher and circuit riding preacher was instrumental in founding the Church and also served as its first pastor.

Jacob Madden was elected to serve as the first Church clerk. The Church held services every other Sunday, as weather permitted, in the old log schoolhouse across Yocum Creek near where the Church building sets today. The seats were made of split chestnut logs, which had been hewn with drawknives and axes. Many times the Church met for their business session on Saturday and preaching would then take up the better part of Sunday morning and afternoon. The Sunday school was established in 1895 and has been maintained from that day on. The Lord continued to bless the congregation and in 1924 it was decided and voted on by the Church to erect a regular house of worship thus leaving the log schoolhouse behind.

A parcel of land was obtained from Brother Baxter Jones and his wife Martha and Brother G.W. Middleton for the purpose of building the new Church building. The first House of God on this site was a large one-room frame structure with the doors facing east looking up Yocum Creek. It had a very high ceiling and was a wide structure. Homemade seats were built of planks with straight backs. The homemade pulpit was moved from the log schoolhouse, as well as other Church property. This building served the growing congregation until it was noticed that the roof was beginning to sag because of the width of the building. Large Poplar poles were placed in the center of the building to help remedy the problem, however, the roof continued to fail and it was decided to tear this building down and replace it.

About 1932, the building was dismantled and a new one room frame Church was constructed. Brother Elijah Creech, a well-known local carpenter, built this House of Worship and it was of good sturdy construction, the doors of this building were placed at the opposite end of the former Church and were now looking west down the creek. The people moved in this building and used it until it was decided in 1947 to build the present building.

The Church at this time was averaging close to two hundred people in Sunday school classes and quite simply had outgrown the old frame House of God. The new building would be of concrete and block and have room for individual Sunday school classes. Brown Brothers and Sons professional carpenters working through Pope Cawood Lumber Company and Supply in Harlan, Kentucky was contracted to build the new Church. Men in the Church spent many hours assisting the carpenters in general labor. As the building progressed, the total expenses for the new Church came to the amount of $11,000.00 dollars, which was entirely paid for by the members of the Church with the attitude of "to God is the glory".

This building is currently still being used. The interior was completely remodeled in 1994 and the exterior being bricked in 1996. Down through the years some great revivals have taken place with services sometimes taking place three times a day and lasting for two weeks or longer. These were known as "Protracted Meetings" and would last until the spirit closed them out. Some of the other great services included the much-anticipated Memorial Day services, which at that time were simply known as "Decoration Day" services. The Decoration Service would move from the House of God to all the local cemeteries for services there. There would usually be a certain tree the preachers would choose to preach the gospel. This tradition of "Homecoming Service" on Memorial Day Saturday and Sunday with a lot of the former residents returning home for this wonderful time of worship.

The Church was at one time also used as the local school house as the log building had fallen into decay. The Church was used until a new schoolhouse was built on Turner's Creek.

Many solid men have served as pastor, William Henry Shoemaker being the founding pastor of the church. Others include J.H. Creech, Jackson Jones, Bill Dean, Ackles Wynn, Clifford Baumgardner, Hurla Phillips and Paul White. Brother Gerald Jones serves as the current pastor and was called to the Church on November 17, 2002.

Thank you for allowing me to include your story in my book Chris.

LOCUST GROVE BAPTIST CHURCH & 1924 OR 1925 CONGREGATION

LOCUST GROVE BAPTIST CHURCH, DIZNEY, KENTUCKY
Late 30s or Early 40s Congregation

6

Dizney Church of God Cemetery List

Allen, Wert, b. 3/28/1908, d. 7/8/1943, Killed in mining accident
Blevins, Dave, NS/DB
Blevins, Dona, b. 7/25/1905, d. 11/6/1947
Blevins, Jim, b. 1/12/1890, d. 10/1951
Blevins, Narcissus, b. 1915, d. 1/5/1966
Blevins, Polly, b. 5/17/1879, d. 4/18/1946
Cloud, B F, b. 9/20/1855, d. 5/1/1945, Son of Benjamin Frank and Nancy Middleton Cloud
Cloud, Cecil, b. 1914, d. 1961, Son of Greenberry Cloud
Cloud, Charlie, b. 4/13/1942, d. 1/10/1965 son of Greenberry Cloud and husband of Etta May Cloud.
Cloud, Etta May, b. 7/18/1891, d. 2/13/1971 wife of Charlie Cloud
Cloud, Frank, b. 11/18/1878, d. 11/25/1962, husband of Mary Jane Cloud
Cloud, H H, b. 9/20/1905, d. 4/12/1922
Cloud, James, b. 8/5/1879, d. 9/27/1930
Cloud, Jeff, b. 1907, d. 1948
Cloud, John A, b. 8/13/1920, d. 4/7/1925
Cloud, Martha L, b. 11/8/1876, d. 4/1/1933, Daughter of William Henry and Elizabeth Redmon Shoemaker
Cloud, Mary Jane, b. 10/15/1889, d. 3/16/1960 wife of Frank Cloud
Cloud, Ova, b. 6/14/1934
Cloud, Pearl, b. 1902, d. 1964—Son of Greenberry Cloud and husband of Tilda
Cloud, Sally, b. 5/28/1915, d. 7/31/1988, wife of Cecil Cloud
Cloud, Sandra b. 2/18/1946 d. 2/19/1946
Cloud, Sarah, b. 3/7/1905, d. 2/28/1938

Cloud, Straley Asberry b. 11/23/1926, d. 5/17/1989, US Navy, Husband of Mildred Haynes Cloud
Cloud, Susie, b. 1/4/1912, d. 2/4/1928
Cloud, Tilda, b. 6/27/1907, d. 2/3/1982 wife of Pearl Cloud
Cloud, Winston, b. 1950, d. 1972, Sarge, killed in car wreck, son of Cecil and Sally Cloud.

Eldridge, Amos, d. 12/24/1926
Elliott, Albert, b. 7/26/1920, d. 12/21/1948
Freeman, Anna Marie, b. 6/22/1965, d. 9/5/1965
Fultz, Haley, b. 8/9/1891, d. 12/26/1889
Gilbert, Brenda Joyce, b. 2/24/1950, d. 2/26/1950
Gilbert, Donald, b. 1936, d. 1937
Gilbert, Jim, b. 9/15/1922, d. 11/24/1976
Gilbert, Sam, b. 1901, d. 1949
Gilbert, Virgie Soloe, b. 11/28/1922, d. 7/8/1979
Hensley, Charles, b. 3/17/1942, d. 11/2/1943
Hensley, Corbin, d. 2/28/1967, age 54
Hensley, James Todd, b. 5/12/1928, d. 4/15/1965
Hensley, Junior, b. 4/21/1934, d. 4/22/1934
Hensley, Noble, b. 5/10/1910, d. 3/30/1965
Hicks, Bige, b. 7/4/1907, d. 2/25/1942
Holman, Donald L, b. 12/1/1936, d. 12/1/1936
Holman, Linda D, b. 1/21/1948, d. 1/30/1948
Holman, Ronald D, b. 12/1/1936, d. 12/1/1936
Johnson, Eva, b. 12/5/1904, d. 8/24/1949, wife of Green Presley
Jones, Baxter, b. 2/8/1883, d. 1/4/1930
Jones, Donnie, b. 3/14/1876, d. 6/21/1911
Jones, Floyd, b. 5/18/1906, d. 3/27/1924
Jones, Jackson Rev., b. 8/5/1881, d. 6/24/1960
Jones, Louisa, b. 5/10/1878, d. 11/28/1913, Wife of JR Jones
Jones, Mary, b. 1/16/1879, d. 4/13/1950, wife of JA Jones, mother-in-law of Isaac Madden
King, Offie Jerome, b. 3/17/1969, d. 3/19/1969
Madden, Dora Thomas, b. 1905, d. 1963,
Madden, Dwight, b. 9/21/1933, d. 8/19/1969, KY Pvt Inf killed in Viet Nam
Madden, E.D., b. 4/2/1909, d. 1/21/1940
Madden, Elkannah, b. 3/24/1861, d. 3/25/1925

Madden, Garland, b. 1904, d. 1925, "killed in mine, buried with Orvill"

Madden, George W, b. 1897, d.,

Madden, Harvey, b. 8/23/1908, d. 11/26/1929

Madden, Henry, b., d. 12/24/1936

Madden, Levy Thomas, b. 1901, d. 1968

Madden, Lige, b. 1876, d. 1968

Madden, Lorraine, b. 9/1/1930, d. 8/2/1958, Daughter of Henry & Roxie

Madden, Nancy Jane, b. 1950, d. 1950, Daughter of Wills & Cedith

Madden, Orvil, b. 1923, d. 1925,

Madden, Rachel, b. 9/26/1889, d. 1/26/1961, Married to Isaac Madden

Madden, Roxie, b. 3/20/1900, d. 11/4/1949, Wife of Henry Madden

McFarland, Albert, b. 7/4/1922, d. 4/26/1945

Middleton, Carr, b. 12/25/1837, d. 12/2/1902

Middleton, James, b. 6/20/1905, d. 7/20/1928

Middleton, Marinda, b. 3/15/1835, d. 10/3/1903

Middleton, Nancy, b. 3/15/1863, d. 10/10/1918

Mullins, Virgil, b. 12/6/1926, d. 12/18/1926

Napier, Fannie, b. 5/21/1900, d. 1981

Pace, Ben, b. 1901, d. 1981, Husband of Lottie Pace

Pace, Claude, b. 12/30/1913, d. 8/22/1934

Pace, Harvey, b. 6/17/1904, d. 5/8/1924

Pace, Henry, b. 3/2/1921, d. 6/14/1950

Pace, Henry, b. 4/28/1875, d. 7/28/1913

Pace, James A, b. 1951, d. 1978, brother of Worley

Pace, Jesse, b. 1/8/1901, d. 2/22/1922

Pace, Jesse, b. 1947, d. 1965, Brother of Vernon, Worley and James

Pace, John A, b. 2/18/1874, d. 3/3/1958

Pace, Lottie, b. 2/6/1902, d. 10/8/1983 Wife of Ben Pace

Pace, Matilda, b. 12/13/1870, d. 9/26/1943

Pace, Vernon, b. 12/2/1942, d. 4/3/1980, Brother of James, Jess and Worley

Pace, Wert Allen, b. 3/28/1908, d. 7/8/1943

Pace, William, b. 9/11/1931, d. 4/21/1987

Pace, Worley, b. 1949, d. 1974, Brother of Jesse, Vernon and James

Presley, Andrew Jackson, b. 10/9/1878, d. 6/12/1924, Husband of Drucilla Presley & son of Archie and Emily Brewer Presley

Presley, Clark, b. 7/16/1920, d. 11/6/1960, Son of Drucilla and Andrew Jackson Presley

Presley, Drusilla, b. 1/30/1882, d. 1/30/1962 Wife of Andrew Jackson Presley, Daughter of Carr Brittain Hall and Julia Ann Lankford Hall

Presley, Elizabeth, b. 6/7/1889, d. 7/7/1956, Wife of Jess Presley Daughter of Archie and Emily Brewer Presley

Presley, Jesse, b. 8/14/1887, d. 3/24/1959, Husband of Elizabeth Wynn Presley, Son of Archie and Emily Brewer Presley

Presley, Maxie, b. 2/16/1915, d. 3/9/1918

Presley, Shelby, b. 1/26/1924, d. 1/7/1955

Thomas, Annie, b. 10/14/1914, d. 3/18/1945, Wife of Earnest Thomes

Thomas, Cora, b. 2/24/1917, d. 1/12/1924

Thomas, Delcie, b. 6/11/1931, d. 12/19/1934

Thomas, Joseph, b. 6/7/1879, d. 7/7/1926, Husband of Laura Napier

Thomas, Laura, b. 1883, d. 1949, Wife of Joseph Thomas

Thomas, Millie, b. 9/1880, d. 3/10/1957, Wife of Sam Thomas

Thomas, Olin, b. 1950, d. 1950

Thomas, Sam, b. 8/21/1874, d. 1/24/1950, Wife of Millie Thomas

Tomlinson, Bryant, b. 8/2/1926, d. 8/3/1926

Tyse, Harvey, b. 2/5/1889, d. 12/8/1947

Winstead, Clarence, b. 12/26/1934, d. 2/14/1936

Winstead, Lucinda, b. 7/9/1882, d. 9/6/1937

Wynn, Ackles, b. 8/1883, d. 7/22/1915

Wynn, Ben, b. 3/2/1887, d. 11/18/1949

Wynn, Bill, b. 3/1/1887, d. 7/26/1939

Wynn, Chester, b. 1918, d. 1/24/1975

Wynn, David, b. 1943, d. 1963

Wynn, Earnest, b. 12/4/1921, d. 1/14/1921

Wynn, Garrett, b. 1909, d. 1962

Wynn, Rhoda, b. 3/11/1866, d. 11/14/1910, Wife of Ackles Wynn

Wynne, B D, b. 3/16/1891, d. 12/23/1942

Wynne, Billie Kay, d. 1929, Baby

7

Turner's Creek Cemetery List

Located in Turner's Creek Holler in Dizney, Kentucky

Blevins, Judy born 5/17/1906 died 6/26/1907 infant
Blevins, Martha born 8/5/1868 died 1/19/1948
Cloud Benjamin Frank born 4/8/1826 in Claiborne, Tennessee, husband of Nancy Middleton Cloud died 8/11/1900 great grandmother of Tilman Cloud, Jr.
Cloud, Baby born 8/31/1899 died 8/31/1899
Cloud, Bessie Colder born 8/26/1925 died 2/26/1927
Cloud, E no dates
Cloud, Jane born 10/1/1870 died 11/11/1940 wife of William Cloud, daughter of William Henry Shoemaker & Elizabeth Redman
Cloud, Jonie born 4/11/1891 died 5/12/1940
Cloud, Nancy born 9/10/1827 died 12/1/1913 wife of Benjamin Frank Cloud III, great grandmother of Tilman Cloud, Jr.
Cloud, Unis Beatris born 3/31/1893 died 9/14/1904
Cloud, William M. born 2/10/1862 died 3/22/1946 husband of Jane Cloud, Son of B. F. and Nancy Middleton Cloud
Holosky, Ballard born 3/5/1930 died 7/29/1951
Holosky, Louis born 8/23/1891 died 2/17/1954
Johnson, M. E. born 6/25/1866 died 8/7/1895
Johnson, M. E. born 6/25/1895 died 10/16/1895
Juat, J. W. born 1903 died 1903 Infant
Middleton, Bill born 4/20/1866 died 1/16/1940
Middleton, Susie born 10/17/1915 died 2/14/1938
Owens, Ballard born 8/16/1898 died 12/8/1922
Pace, Howard born 1/26/1859 died 9/20/1907
Shoemaker, Joseph born 3/10/1843 died 12/20/1911

Thomas, Bobby Reed born4/22/1942 died 11/9/1961
Thomas, Cudge no dates
Thomas, Elmon born 12/27/1937 died 7/16/1985
Thomas, Eugene born 7/7/1930 died2/4/1963
Thomas, J. D. born 1/22/1919 died 1/22/1919 Infant
Thomas, Sarah no dates
Webb, Floyd born 8/4/1904 died 2/17/1939
Wynn, J. Morgan born 3/1864 died 3/1900
Wynn, Larina born 4/10/1847 died 3/7/1878
Wynn, Nancy born 10/17/1867 died 8/21/1896

8

Jones/White Oak Cemetery List

On Yokum Creek, Dizney, Kentucky

Blevins, Infant no dates
Cornett, Infant 10/30/1956 died 10/30/1956
Gibb, Infant no dates
Hensley, Larry, Jr. born 9/19/1962 died 12/22/1962 Infant
Jones, Edborn 1848 died 1924
Jones, Ewell born 7/26/1904 died 3/19/1957
Jones, Fanny born 11/15/1886 died 9/5/1952
Jones, Fielden born 12/1/1877 died 7/6/1933
Jones, John born 2/3/1881 died 3/10/1960
Jones, Juanita born 1/25/1923 died 8/18/1980
Jones, Martha born 1855 died 1935
Jones, Oalun born 1888 died 1955
Jones, Washington born 4/13/1906 died 3/18/1955
Pace, Clarence born 3/22/1940died 6/29/1959
Pace, George W. born 3/1/1879 died 10/15/1957
Pace, Harvey born 1911 died 1969
Pace, Lee born 3/4/1909 died 1/15/1968
Pace, Lessie born 10/27/1904 died 3/5/1987
Pace, Luther no dates
Pace, Minnie no dates
Pace, Ulysses BORN 6/1/1931 DIED 2/17/1967
Thompson, Dave born 5/27/1920 died 4/6/1970
Thomspson, Deltia born 6/21/1906 died 6/17/1980
Thompson, Harman born 3/22/1911 died 2/6/1955
Thompson, John born 8/24/1884 died 1/4/1961

9

Thirty One Cemetery List

Just past Kenvir on the right hand side of Highway 215 before Dizney.

Barnes, Pearl O born 10/16/1861 died 1887
Barnes, Roy born 12/25/1906 died 7/16/1944
Blair, Doxie G. born 3/30/1892 died 12/5/1923
Blevins, Clemont born 2/24/1917 died 9/2/1980
Blevins, Hiram born 10/28/1894 died 7/7/1950
Blevins, Peggy born 7/15/1847 died 7/16/1926
Clark, Kenneth E. born 3/20/1950 died 11/29/1970
Daniels, Alaberta born 11/28/1908 died 3/30/1940 Tilman Cloud's sister
Davix, Lora born 4/19/1903 died 4/30/1954
Davis, Roy born 12/15/1891 died 10/12/1967
Duff, W. L. born 10/29/1859 died 12/19/1932
Eugene, George born 3/20/1933 died 9/14/1940
Fraley, Ann born 1948 died 1954
Gilbert, Della Thomas born 1900 died 10/13/1970
Gilbert, Emily born 9/22/1912 died 4/23/1941
Gilbert, Mary Jane born 1876 died 1960
Gilliam, Larry Bernard born 11/24/1947 died 12/17/1947 Infant
Greene, Pattie M. born 1917 died 1950
Griffith, Fred born 9/9/1925 died 6/25/1926
Griffith, Sarah born 1871 died 1957
Hale, James W. born 11/2/1902 died 10/16/1982 my grandfather
Hale, Rebecca born 4/30/1903 died 1995 my grandmother
Hall, Nathan E. born 8/19/1907 died 5/18/1955
Hammock, Charles T. born 3/5/1902 died9/18/1960
Hayes, Lela born 2/19/1910 died?
Hayes, Rev born 11/5/1906 died 1/30/1978

Helton, Otis born 7/26/1924 died 1/11/1952
Helton, Serepta born 1/1/1988 died 10/2/1957
Hensley, Dave born 7/4/1894 died 5/23/1966
Hensley Elizabeth born 8/11/1901 died 8/9/1965
Hensley, Josephine born 12/24/1898 died 2/22/1965
Hensley, Sam born 1875 died 1952
Hoover, Howard H. born 1917 died 1939
Hoover, Iris I born? died 1919
Howard, Oscar S. born 1910 died 1949
Johnson, Cecil H. born 1880 died 7/23/1936
Johnson, Dillard born 4/7/1898 died 11/21/1958
Johnson, Edd born 10/14/1885 died 1/24/1959
Johnson, F. F. born 1853 died 1925
Johnson, Lloyd S. born 9/29/1898 died 11/7/1957
Jones, David J. born 1921 died 1937
Jones, Hattie E born 1894 died 1959
Kelly, Charles A. born 11/19/1884 died 6/12/1930
Lamb, Henry P. born 1961 died 4/4/1966
Lamb, John, JR. born 1950 died 4/4/1966
Lamb, Lilly born 1944 died 4/4/1966
Lamb, Sherrie born 1963 died 1963
Lockhart, James born 3/4/1900 died 6/10/1969
Lockhart, Larry born 2/2/1950 died 10/21/1950
Lockhart, Otis, born 12/24/1907 died 11/17/1956
Madden, Champ born 5/8/1820 died 11/17/1898
Madden, Isaac born 3/27/1864 died 4/3/1949
Madden, Isaac born 4/10/1929 died 10/2/1953
Mall, Delty born 5/10/1910 died 8/18/1986
Messer, Johnny born 3/28/1931 died 9/5/1931
Middleton, Celieorn 9/28/1902 died 10/26/1942
Middleton, Drucilla born 3/2/1880 died 4/26/1936
Middleton, Kerby born 4/3/1905 died 10/6/1939
Middleton, Lawrence born 6/21/1907 died 8/29/1943
Middleton, Samuel H. born 7/14/1848 died 7/12/1928
Mulkins, Louis born 1927 died 1950
Nunley, Alex born 5/11/1891 died 3/20/1963
Parsons, Emma born 1879 died 1966
Partin, Sylvester born 3/5/1901 died 2/10/1959

Price, Christine Louise born 8/17/1938 died 12/4/1956
Rainey, Dillard born 1932 died 1935
Rainey, James J. born 1900 died 1945
Rainey, Jerline born 1934 died 1934 infant
Schulte, Edward L. born 9/25/1934 died 4/15/1982
Schulte, Thelma C. born 5/31/1929 died?
Sester, John born 4/21/1917 died 12/28/1965
Sester, Rosa G. born 4/7/1912 died 4/29/1985
Smith, John born 10/12/1871 died 1/8/1950
Smith, Pearle born 7/19/1867 died 10/17/1924
Thomas, James B. born 6/7/1867 died 10/17/1924
Thomas, Lawrence, born 5/16/1912 died 4/1/1987
Thomas, Louise born 5/22/1904 died 3/14/1968
Thomas, Mary 1/4/1879 died 4/20/1924
West, James Riley born 10/1/1926 died 10/21/1926 Infant
West, Yvonne born? died 7/27/1935
Williams, James born? died 4/29/1930
Willis, Alice Gilbert born 1916 died 6/13/1969
Willis, George W. born 1914 died 1954

10

The Cloud Family

No stories have ever been written about my Appalachian Mountain family. in the southeast corner of Kentucky that borders Tennessee and Virginia, that I know of. My ancestors came from Lee County, Virginia, which in the 1700s included a portion that was to become Tennessee. Some of my ancestors who are listed in the census of northwestern North Carolina and southwestern Virginia, actually lived not far from each other as the land in this portion of the Appalachian Mountains belonged to Virginia in the late 1700s, but later became a part of Eastern Tennessee.

The settlers of this region came through the Cumberland Gap in Virginia or Bonnie Blue Mountain which bordered Virginia and Kentucky at the head of Dizney, Kentucky, to what they hoped would be a better future for their families.

There are several members of my ancestral family tree that crossed paths in Lee County, Virginia. The Chadwell Family, Brittain Family, Middleton Family, Wynn and Cloud Family were pioneers from Lee County, Virginia. The Chadwells built a fort or stockade in Lee County, Virginia which was used for protection for the surrounding families from the Indians and where pioneers stopped to rest before traveling on to the Cumberland Gap into Kentucky. The Cloud family descendants were:

1. Benjamin Franklin Cloud I(William H. Cloud V, William IV, William III, Jeremiah, William I) born about 1777 in Tennessee died 1845, married Mary (Polly) Chadwell born 1777, daughter of David Chadwell and Elizabeth Turner on December 19, 1801. Note that Mary (Polly) Chadwell was first married to Walter Middleton, Sr. (grandfather of Nancy Middleton).

Children of Benjamin Franklin Cloud 1, born about 1777 and Mary (Polly) Chadwell are:

Benjamin Franklin Cloud II or Jr. born November 8, 1802 in Hawkins, Tennessee

Barthena Cloud born May 5, 1804, married Josiah R. Smith

Nancy Cloud married Gabriel Shackleford

Louisana Cloud born about 1810 married Jacob Shultz, Jr.

Elizabeth Cloud born January 10, 1814

2. Benjamin Franklin Cloud II (BF Cloud I, William H Cloud, V, William IV, Jeremiah, William I) was born 1802 in Hawkins County, Tennessee, died 1880 in Tazewell, Claiborne County, TN

He married (1) Elizabeth Chadwell, daughter of John Chadwell and married (2) Elizabeth Mahulda Shultz.

Children of Benjamin Frank Cloud II born 1802 and Elizabeth Chadwell are:

Benjamin Franklin (Frank) Cloud born 1826 Claiborne County, TN

Elizabeth Cloud born 1829 Claiborne County, TN

Children of Benjamin Franklin Cloud II born 1802 and Elizabeth Mahulda Shultz are:

Alexander Moore Cloud born 1847 died 1925

Merander Cloud born 1847

Benjamin Franklin Cloud born 1849 died 1850

Carrack Cloud born 1854

Benjamin F and Elizabeth Mahulda Schultz lived in Claiborne County, Tennessee. Their son Alexander Moore Cloud was a writer and wrote some stories of Tazwell, Tennessee.

3. Benjamin Franklin (Frank) Cloud III, son of BF Cloud and Elizabeth Chadwell, (B.F. Jr., B.F. I, William H. V, William IV, William III, Jeremiah, William I) born 1826 in Claiborne County, TN, died about 1900 in Dizney, Harlan County, KY. He married (1) Nancy Middleton on May 12, 1850 in Claiborne County, TN, daughter of Walter Middleton and Sarah Turner. He married (2) Margaret Jane Ayers on May 31, 1870 in Lee County, VA.

Children of Benjamin Franklin (Frank) Cloud and Nancy Jane Middleton were:
Alexander born 1852, Claiborne County, TN married Nancy Jane Burkhart.
Greenberry born 1854, Claiborne County, TN married Clara Goodwin.
Their children were:

Frank Cloud b. about 1885 in Harlan, Kentucky, married Mary Jane Wynn about 1899 in Kentucky
Their children were:
1)Homer Cloud born 2/9/1919 in Dizney, Kentucky, died 12/1/2002 Lexington, Indiana, married Mary Ellen Brewer Cloud
2)Pearl Cloud born 8/8/1901 in Dizney, Kentucky, married Tilde
3)Sarah Cloud
4)Jesse Cloud born 1907 in Dizney, Kentucky
5)Simon Cloud born 9/7/1909 in Dizney, Kentucky
6)Charley Cloud born 4/14/1912 died 1/1965 in Dizney, Kentucky, married Eddie Mae
7)Cecil Cloud born 10/31/1914 died 1961 in Dizney, Kentucky
8)Rebecca Cloud born? Dizney, Kentucky
9)Emiline Cloud born 3/10/1917 Dizney Kentucky

Benjamin F. Cloud born 1855 in Claiborne County, TN married Martha Shoemaker on 8/30/1897

Their children were:
1)Tilman Cloud born 1901 in Dizney, Kentucky died 1970 in Dizney, Kentucky, married to Leona Presley Cloud
Harrison Cloud,
Octavia
Ida
Mary E. born 1857 Claiborne County TN
James born 1859 Harlan County, KY married Rebecca Browning
William born 1862 Harlan County, KY
Shelby Longstreet born 1865 Harlan County, KY married Bettie Nolen on 12/18/1902
Sarah born 1868 Harlan County Kentucky

Children of Benjamin Franklin (Frank) Cloud and Margaret Jane Ayers are:

Elizabeth (Lizzy)
Virginia (Jenny) married Jackson Edds
Margaret V. born June 7, 1875 in Lee County, VA
Mary A. born June 7, 1875 in Lee County, VA
Serelda, Cornie & Dora

Frank is found again with Nancy in Kentucky in the 1880 Census of Harlan County, KY District #12. I believe that sometime prior to 1880 he left Margaret Jane Ayers and moved to Harlan County, KY where he rejoined Nancy. They continued to own the farm in Lee County, VA. Later, his son William returned to live on the farm in Lee County, VA and raised his family there. Benjamin Franklin Cloud died in Harlan County, KY.

The Harlan County, KY 1880 census lists him as follows:

Frank Cloud, age 55 b. KY(incorrect, was born in Tennessee)
Nancy age 53 born in KY
Green age 26, born in KY (incorrect, was born in Tennessee)
James age 21 born in KY
Bill age 18 born in KY
Shelby age 15 born in KY
Sarah age 12 born in KY
Frank (grandson) age 2 born in KY (See your notes #653
Also, Yokums Creek, Mag. Dist 2, Harlan County, KY 1900 Census which lists family as follows:
Benjamin F. Cloud born April 1826, TN age 74
Nancy (wife) born September 1827 KY age 72
Benjamin F. (grandson) born October 1879 KY age 22
James (grandson) born August 1879 age 20

Benjamin F. Cloud Jr or II held the following public offices in Claiborne County Tennessee, along with David Chadwell:

Claiborne County Clerk—Benjamin F. Cloud from 1816 to 1836
Claiborne County Clerk—David Chadwell from 1862 to 1862 (Probably a cousin to his wife)
Clerks of the Superior Court: Jermiah Cloud 1815 to 1826
Clerks of the Superior Court: Benjamin F. Cloud 1836 to 2844

I have a copy of a printed statement that refers to the father of the first Benjamin Franklin Cloud who married Mary Chadwell (Middleton) Cloud. I am so excited because I now know his father's name was William born 1750 died 1842 married to Mary Elizabeth (Morgan) Cloud.

Their children were:

1) Benjamin Franklin Cloud born around 1775 (other papers say 1777) died 1845 married Mary Chadwell Middleton.
2) Jeremiah Cloud born 1/21/1781 died 1829 married Karen Berry
3) Greenberry Cloud born 1781 went to Tazwell, Tennessee (It is possible that Jeremiah and Greenberry were twins)
4) Joseph Cloud married Nancy Moore, went to Kentucky
5) George Washington Cloud born 1798 died 1846 married Lucinda Walker
6) Samuel Cloud married Margaret?
7)Betty Cloud married a Mr. Carlin and lived and died in Grayson County, Virginia
7) Polly Cloud married Jim Hussey and lived in Texas

Most of Dizney, Kentucky's ancestors came from Pennsylvania and Delaware where some fought in the War for Independence. They traveled to Eastern Virginia and there fought in the war of 1812. Cumberland Gap was a famous trail leading from southwestern Virginia to Southeastern Kentucky. There was another mountain range that was called "Bonnie Blue" that bordered Kentucky and Virginia just above Dizney, Kentucky. Most of our ancestors came to Kentucky via either of these two routes.

In the 1800s many people came to Dizney using this route. They also crossed back over Bonnie Blue to trade, work and visit family in Virginia.

Each branch or holler of Yokum Creek (Dizney, Kentucky) had its own name. These names were usually named for the first settlers. There was Cloud's Branch, Jones Creek, Turner's Creek, Bills Creek and Stretchneck Holler. No one knows when Stretchneck holler was named or how it got its name.

The father of Benjamin Franklin Cloud, husband of Nancy Middleton Cloud, lived in Claiborne County, Kentucky. His second wife was Elizabeth Schultz. Benjamin Franklin Cloud II started a new family with his second wife. He and his family continued to live in Claiborne County, Kentucky. Benjamin F. Cloud II became a political figure in local politics. His son Alexander Moore Cloud became a prolific writer. He wrote about the history of Old Time Tazwell, Tennessee.

BENJAMIN FRANKLIN CLOUD III

LONGSTREET, BEN, WILLIAM, ALEXANDER & SARAH
CLOUD

11

English Settlers among the Germans and Swiss

An article found on the internet regarding the Brief History of Lancaster County, Pennsylvania.

In 1715 some English and Welsh settlers came and located around Smoketown. The names of these were Peter Bellas, Daniel Harman, William Evans and James Smith. In 1716 Richard Carter, an Englishman, took up a tract of land between the Conestoga and Pequea creeks, near the Susquehanna River, and therefore in the present Conestoga township. In the same year other English settlers took up tracts on the south side of the Conestoga. The names of these were Alexander Bews, Anthony Pretter of East Jersey and John Gardiner of Philadelphia County, Pennsylvania. In 1717 Joseph Cloud secured 500 acres near the Pequea.

12

The Chester County, Pennsylvania Cloud Connection

Edward Beeson b. 1652 Lancaster, England died 1712–1713 in Chester County, Pennsylvania.

The first member of the family to arrive was Edward Beeson, along with his wife Rachel Pennington.

Edward Beeson and his wife, Rachel, came into the colonies by way of a land grant from William Penn, a Quaker. This is the same way the Cloud ancestors came into the colonies via William Penn. It is not known if the Beesons were Quakers. However, it is known that they lived in Chester County, Pennsylvania.

The GenWeb page, had this exciting picture layout of the early town (1702). If you look closely at the top left of the picture, you can see Edward Beeson's name on his piece of property in the town of East Nottingham. (picture not included).

The parentage of Rachel Pennington has been argued as long as there have been Beeson family researchers. Perhaps, someday, we will know more about Rachel, but for now we must be content with the knowledge that she was there to help found this well known family.

The children of Edward and Rachel Beeson

1) Edward Beeson b. abt. 1681, W. Nottingham, Chester Co., PA died 1725 married to Esther Hall in 1703 at Newark, PA Meeting of the Society of Friends

2) Isaac Beeson is a second son introduced in Jasper Luther Beeson's book on the family and repeated in the new Beeson Genealogy revised by James Dawson and published in 1997. Isaac (according to these sources) married Ann Cloud and moved near Orange County, NC prior to the death (and will) of his father. Dawson's book includes a fair-sized chapter on his family.

3) William Martin Beeson b. 1690 married (2nd) Ann Bennett. William returned to England after a brief stay in the colonies.

4) Anne Beeson married John Cloud, son of William Cloud.

This information was found through my search of the Morman Genealogy Site.

13

David Chadwell

David Chadwell, Sr. is the father of Mary Polly Chadwell Cloud who married the first Benjamin Franklin Cloud. This history was written by one of his Virginia descendants and given to Helen Presley who gave a copy to me.

David Chadwell, Sr. was born in England in 1732, and migrated to America with his parents. The emigrant Chadwell ancestors are of record in King George and Stafford Counties, Virginia in the early 1720s. The first record of David Chadwell was in Halifax and Pittsylvania Counties and later in Henry County, Virginia in 1752. David was nominated as officer in the militia February 27, 1775, and served in the Revolutionary War with the rank of Captain.

David and Elizabeth Chadwell sold their land holding in Pittsylvania County, Virginia and moved to Lee County, Virginia in 1790. Captain Chadwell acquired by deed a 400 acre tract of land and another 707 acres from the heirs of Mordecai Hoard, deeds to the tracts being dated November 1791. The records show that David Chadwell was in Powell Valley before the deeds of the land sales were recorded. David Chadwell came to Powell Valley in southwestern Virginia about 1780 where he built the "Old Block House" called Chadwell Station, in honor of his family. This was a refuge from Indian attacks for Chadwell and his neighbors as well as a stop-over for weary pioneers traveling westward. Eventually, a church was established called "Chadwell Station". Captain David Chadwell was a member of the Houses of Delegates in 1794–1795. David continued to acquire land in both Lee County and adjoining Claiborne County in Tennessee. He made gifts of land to his sons and sons-in-law, these deeds all of record in Lee County, Virginia. David Chadwell and his wife, Elizabeth had the following children:

1) John born 1771
2) Susannah born 1772
3) Nancy born 1774
4) Barthena born 1775
5) Mary Polly born 1777
6) William born 1779
7) David, Jr born 1781
8) Alexander born 1783

David Chadwell married a second time in his old age and had a son, Jack born after 1871. David Chadwell moved with his young son to Claiborne County, Tennessee, and settled in Tazewell where he died in 1832 at the age of 100. He is buried in Tazwell on Breastwork Hill.

14

The Wynn Family of Dizney

Acles Wynn was born December 20, 1798 in Lee County Virginia and died about 1861. The elder Acles Wynn was a preacher. The name Acles was passed down through the generations of Wynn family.

The older brother of Acles Wynn, Wright Wynn, was born in 1820. He married Joanna Middleton, daughter of Walter and Sara Turner Middleton. Wright and Joanna were first cousins. They had eleven children. This family must have lived in Yokum Creek (Dizney) as they married into families already living in the hollers of Dizney. Lucy married Ramson Blevins. The Blevins family lived in Bills Creek. Mary married David Jones. The Jones families lived in Yokum Creek holler. Benjamin married Emily Blevins. Judith married Benjamin F. Cloud. His family lived on Cloud branch off Yokum Creek holler. Morgan married Nancy Shoemaker. Wynn and Pace families also married each other. Elizabeth Wynn married Jess Presley brother to Andrew Jackson Presley. Mary Jane Wynn married Frank Cloud, son of Greenberry Cloud.

15

The Brittain Family

Sir William Brittain lived on the Isle of Brittain in the 11th Century. When the Isle was invaded by the Normans, he was driven to the mountains of Wales. There his descendants lived until the 18th century when James Brittain, a lineal descendant of Sir William and a collateral descendant of William (the Norman) decided to leave Wales and come to America.

James Brittain settled first in Virginia and then went to North Carolina. He had several sons, all of whom were prominent in the Revolutionary War. These seven sons were Joseph, Benjamin, James, William, Nathaniel, Enoch and Samuel.

Nathan Brittain was born before 1740, he was James Brittain's fifth son, and to whom we trace our lineage. He married Elizabeth Parks and later enlisted in the Revolutionary War. He served as Captain in Jonathan Clarks Company, Eighth Virginia Regiment.

George Brittain second child of Nathaniel and Elizabeth Brittain was born in 1768 and died in 1848. George Brittain married twice, first to Mary Baily, and then to Nancy Posey. The children of George and Mary were: George, Jr. b. 1798, Carr b. 1800, James b. 1802, Sarah b 1804, Nancy b 1806 and Elizabeth b 1808. Children of George and his second wife, Nancy Posey Brittain, were Carlo b 1819 d 1888, Louisa b 1822 d 1882 and Drucilla b 1826 d 1865.

George, Jr. settled on Martins Fork, Kentucky. This is land that was a part of the Skidmore farm of today. He was the county clerk and prominent in other affairs of the county. He owned a number of slaves which were among the first ever used in this section of Kentucky.

Carr Brittain, son of George, had two daughters. They were Julie Ann and Lucy Ann. My great grandmother is traced through both of Carr Brittians daughters. Julie Ann Brittain married Benjamin Lankford. Lucy Ann Brittain married William T. Hall. Their son Carlo Brittain Hall married the daughter of Julie Ann and Benjamin Lankford, her name was also Julie Ann. Their daughter was Drucilla Hall who married Andrew Jackson Presley my great grandparents.

Carr Brittain Hall was married to a Lankford and a Ledford. It is confusing. His marriage to Julie Ann Lankford ended in divorce.

16

William Henry Shoemaker

This written history of Reverend Shoemaker was given to my father by his cousin whose mother was a sister to Tilman Cloud Sr. Reverend Shoemaker and his family settled in Yokum Creek and his daughters married into family already living in this tiny community.

William Henry Shoemaker was born July 10, 1842 in Alleghany County, Virginia. He was the son of John K.E. Shoemaker and Elizabeth Matthews Shoemaker, daughter of Thomas Matthews. Some time after 1852 William's mother Elizabeth died and by 1860 William was bonded out to a John Callaghan. It is not known what caused the separation of his father and William. William was being mistreated by Mr. Callaghan so he ran away.

The next record of William who usually went by the name of Henry, is when he enlisted in the Confederate Army at Hickey Flats, Virginia in November 1862. Henry was shortly promoted to Sargent in Company C of the 64th Regiment Virginia Mounted Infantry. Henry was later found at Cumberland Gap Tennessee when his commander, being under the influence of a large quantity of liquor surrendered to the Union Forces.

Henry Shoemaker and the other prisoners were sent to a Union military prison in Louisville, Kentucky. From Louisville they were moved to Camp Douglas in Chicago, Illinois. Henry remained at Camp Douglas until the war ended.

According to information given to the Upper Cumberland Association of Harlan County, Kentucky to be used for a Memorial Edition for William Shoemaker after his death, it was while he was in the army that he was converted to Christianity on March 24, 1863 at Chicago. He met John H. Redman from Scott County, Virginia and they became very good friends.

When the war ended Henry Shoemaker had no where to go home to so he was invited by John Redman to come home with him. Henry and Elizabeth, John's sister, were married on December 10, 1866. Elizabeth was the daughter of Andrew Jackson Redman and Elizabeth Jones Redman. Andrew Jackson Redman performed the vows of matrimony for William and Elizabeth.

Henry and Elizabeth Shoemaker lived for some time in Scott County, Va., and Lee County, Virginia. They then moved to Harlan County, Kentucky about 1881 or 1882. William bought land on December 4, 1882 from Calvin and Lavina Pace and Isaac Huff on Yokum Creek of the Cloverfork branch of the Cumberland River. He later sold this land to John B. Lewis in June 1904. On August 9, 1904 William purchased from W. B. and Sally Ball a portion of the land on Four Mile Creek.

William was a Baptist minister and faithful to his calling. On March 17, 1890, he was a member of the Presbyterian of the convention being held at Mount Pleasant Baptist Church in Harlan, Kentucky where they organized "The Upper Cumberland Association of Baptists." The Historical Records of the Association from the years 1890–1911 show that William Shoemaker was the Moderator six times and preached the Introductory Serman ten times for the annual meetings.

The Locust Grove Baptist Church was established in 1885. Henry Shoemaker served as its first pastor. In 1887, William Henry Shoemaker became the pastor of the Mt. Pleasant Baptist Church and remained pastor until 1889. He also was the pastor at the Four Mile Baptist Church as well as preached at many other churches. Many times William and Elizabeth would ride their big black horses through the mountains to preach the gospel.

There are many stories told by grandchildren of William that he had been passed on from their parents. One such story goes that one time William rode his horse over Pine Mountain to preach. He had preached several times at this one church and had received no pay in offerings. Upon returning this time, when he stepped up to the pulpit he made the statement "No pay—no preach". Another time he had preached and after the service was invited to a home to have dinner. The lady of the house said "Come and sit down but it ain't fit for a dog". To which William replied "If it ain't fit for a dog, it ain't fit for me". And he refused to eat.

Once when William went to preach at a church, it had rained all day and was still raining that evening. Time came for church and one man showed up. William was not going to preach but the man said "Yes you are going to preach, I traveled a long way through the mountains to hear you preach." William preached and the man was saved. After that William would say "That was one time I preached and the whole house was saved.

On the day of his death, March 24, 1912, William got up that morning and told his family that he had a strange dream the night before. In the dream, he saw a man who walked across the room and stopped at the door. When he went through the door, he fell and died. Later that evening about dark, William got up to go out on the front porch and as he went through the door he collapsed. By the time members of the family had reached him he had already died. The following are children of Henry and Elizabeth Shoemaker shows how the Dizney families intermarried.

The children of William Henry and Elizabeth Redmond Shoemaker were:

1. Nancy Elizabeth Shoemaker was born 10/17/1867 in Scott County, Va. She died 8/21/1896 in Harlan County, Kentucky. Nancy married Morgan Wynn who was born in Harlan, Ky on 12/25/1864 and died 8/1900.

Their Children were:
1a) Mary Jane Wynn born November 1883, married 9/11/1900 to Frank Cloud
1b) James Wynn born May 1885, married Annie Engle or Engram
1c) Elizabeth Wynn born 9/7/1889, married Jess Presley, died 7/7/1956
1d) William Henry Wynn born 3/1893 married Ollie Carter, died 3/4/1964
1e) Acles Wynn born 11/22/1893, married Delia J. Thomas, who died 12/18/1979. He was a Baptist preacher and pastured at Brittains Creek and Dizney Baptist churches.
1f) Benjamin Wynn born 3/2/1887
1g) Joanna Wynn born 1889 married Wash (Washington?) Cloud

2. William Jackson Shoemaker born 1/11/1869, in Scott County, Virginia died 6/15/1945 in Springfield, Mo. married to Narcissus Middleton born 1/27/1875 and died 8/15/1950 Culver City, Calif.

Their children were:

2a) Joseph born 3/10/1893 died at a young age.

2b) Luther B. born 12/9/1895, died 9/17/1948 married Lois?.

2c) Henry Clay born 5/6/1900, died at a young age.

2d) William Ray born 2/18/1902, died 11/16/81 married Cora C. Reary.

2e) Robert L. born 10/5/1905, married Velma Hatfield.

2f) Claude D. Born 10/16/1908 died 9/2/42 serving in WWII

3. Mary Jane Shoemaker born 10/1/1870, Scott County, Va died 11/11/1940 Harlan County, Ky., married William M. Cloud (brother of Benjamin Franklin Cloud) born 2/20/1862 died in Harlan County, Ky. on 3/22/1946.

Their children were:

3a) Henry F. Cloud born 4/30/1893 died 9/5/1968, married Sybil Sweeter.

3b) Greenberry Cloud born 2/4/1895 died 11/22/1960, married Bertha Middleton.

3c) Unis Beatrice Cloud born 3/13/1898 died 9/14/1904.

3d) Louisa M. Cloud born 8/23/1900 died 1/8/1986, married Frank Russell.

3e) Laura Belle Cloud born 11/3/1907, married Floyd Webb.

3f) Serepta Cloud born 1/4/1906 died 1/8/1986, married Hobart Short.

3g) Alice Cloud born 11/15/1907??, married Floyd Webb.

3h) John Evan Cloud born 7/23/1910 died 8/1979, married Virgie Woodward.

3i) Bessie Cloud born 10/1/1912, married Willie Madden

4. John Robert Shoemaker born 8/18/1872 in Lee County, Va, died 10/24/1959 in Harlan County Kentucky. He married Manerva Middleton born 1/1/1879 and died 1/16/196? in Harlan County, Ky.

Their children were:

4a) Henry born 8/13/1892, died young

4b) Elizabeth born 11/12/1894 died 8/14/1979, never married

4c) George born 3/3/1896, died young

4d) Luther born 1/18/1898, married to Nettie Farley, died 7/9/1936

4e) Ludie born 10/9/1881

5. James Thomas Shoemaker born 8/29/1874 Lee County, Va., died 9/14/1926 in Harlan County Kentucky. He married (1) Maebelle Waddell, (2) Mary Noe.

(1)
Their children were:
5a) Paul b 1901
5b) Earl b 1903 d 1938
5c) Ocie b 8/19/1905 d 8/15/1927
(2)
Their children were:
5d) Ray b 8/4/1916 m Bertha M. Reed; d 11/21/1974
Ina b 1/7/1918 md Tony H. Dietrich
Henry b 6/25/1920 md Juanita Hayes

6. Martha L. Shoemaker born 11/28/1876 in Lee County Va. Died 4/1/1933 in Harlan County Kentucky, married Benjamin Frank Cloud III

Their children were:

6a) Josephine b. 7/1898 d. 1917
6b) Tilman Cloud b. 1/23/1901 md Leona Presley; d. 1/7/1972
6c) Ida B. Cloud b. 1903 md Steve Cherko
6d) Harrison Cloud b 11/14/1904 md. Cora Johnson d.
6e) Matilda Cloud b. 1906 md. Shelby Daniels; d
6f) Alberta Cloud b. 1908 md Bascom Daniels; d 1940
6g) Doxie Cloud b 7/16/1912 md Archie Harris d
6h) Octavia Cloud b 4/1914 md Eulyses Emmett d

7. King Hezekiah Shoemaker born 2/22/1879 in Lee County, Va; died 10/23/1958 in Harlan County Kentucky; married (1) Ida E. Johnson (2) Hazel Mooney.

(1)
Their children were:
7a) Monroe b 1/15/1904; md Bessie Gadd; d. 6/16/1955
7b) Thelma b 4/1/1906; md Verlin Robbins; d 1/3/1964

7c) Hazel b 12/23/1907; md Herbert Rice; d 4/19/1974
7d) Victor B. b 11/18/1909; md Ruth?; d 3/28/1977
7e) Ruby b 2/22/1912; md Thomas C. Summers; d
7f) Augustus b 10/16/1916; md Elizabeth Kelly; d 9/19/1974
7g) Lorraine b 9/9/1924; md Luster Otis Cottrell; d

(2)
Their children were:
7h) King H. Jr. b. 1/20/1933 d
7i) Willis Charles b 1/7/1935 d 6/5/1983
7j) Buford Wayne b 9/6/1937 d
7k) Daniel b 11/16/1939 d 10/15/1940
7l) Donald b 11/16/1939 d
7m) Basil Clark b 6/5/1943

8. Henry Benson Shoemaker b. 4/16/1881 in Lee County Va; died 5/19/1956 in Harlan County Kentucky; married (1) Laura C. Waddell (2) Maude Kelly.

(1)
Their children were:
8a) Willie B. b? d 5/1931
8b) Golden b? md John Lawson d
(2)
Their children were:
8c) Hubert B. b 6/12/1912; md Lavina Pace; d 11/23/19?
8d) Lucy b 9/28/1915; md Dudley Baute; d 1/12/1987
8e) Neil b 10/20/1919; md Arnold Hayes, Sr.; d
8f) Lois b 5/14/1935; md Lloyd Napier; d

9. Drucilla R. Shoemaker b 3/2/1883 in Harlan County Kentucky; died 4//26/1936; married James T. Middleton.

Their children were:
9a) Laura b 1900
9b) Celia b 1902
9c) Kirby b 1904
9d) Lawrence b 1906

9e) Elizabeth b 1910
9f) Emily b? md Joe Gilbert

10. Lucy A. Shoemaker b 7/8/1885 in Harlan County Kentucky; died 5/2/1926 in Harlan County Kentucky; married Speed B. Irvin.

Their children were:
10a) Shafter b 4/2/1922 d?
10b) Elva Elizabeth b 4/12/1926; d 10/23/1926

11. Sarepta A. Shoemaker born 1/1/1888 in Harlan County Kentucky; died 10/10/1957 Kingsport, Tennessee; married James Allen Helton.

Their children were:
11a) Nobe b 10/17/1914 md Jean? d
11b) Marie b 6/5/1917 md? Blair
11c) Lige b 3/6/1921 d
11d) Otis 7/26/1924 d 1/11/1953
11e) Drucilla b 1/11/1926 md Riley Causey; d
11f) Victoria b 7/29/1930 md Jess Smith

Preacher Shoemaker established Locust Grove Missionary Baptist Church and preached in this church until his death. At which time Brother Jackson Jones took over as the pastor.

This biography was done by the children of Ida Cloud Cherako, sister to Tilman Cloud Sr.

WILLIAM HENRY SHOEMAKER

17

Benjamin Franklin and Nancy Middleton Cloud

Ben Frank and Nancy Cloud lived on top of the mountain in Cloud's Branch, Yokum Creek, Dizney, Kentucky. They were self sufficient in that they hunted for meat and grew their own vegetables. All clothes and quilts were homemade. They built their log cabin and barns for their animals. Ben Frank was a black smith and made the tools that were needed by his family. They only came off the mountain a few times a year.

As the children grew up they ended up marrying close cousins because the people living in the area were isolated and did not have the means to travel to other communities. Going to the county seat in Harlan was an all day trip on horse and wagon. The Wynn, Cloud, Blevins, Shoemaker, Middleton, Thomas and Jones families intermarried. Some of Ben Frank and Nancy's sons moved out of Dizney to start their families around Evarts and in the area of Harlan. Three of the brothers stayed in Dizney. William, Greenberry and Benjamin Franklin's family lived in Yokum Creek.

Benjamin Franklin Cloud married Judith Wynn. Their children were Nancy, James and Delilah. Ben and a friend of his were framed for murder and were sent to prison for life. While Ben was in prison Judith became pregnant with another man's child.

After spending ten years in prison, the man who was responsible for bribing people to give false testimony at the trial confessed and the Supreme Court of Kentucky pardoned the two men. When Ben came home and found Judith with another man's child he divorced her.

The Cloud boys acquired property on the tops of the mountains in Dizney. Benjamin Franklin was a farmer and blacksmith by trade. Ben met Martha Shoemaker, probably at a church service, and they were married.

Their children were: Josephine, Tilman Thomas, Ida Bell, Harrison, Matilda, Alberta and Octavia.

The girls eventually married and moved out of Dizney and then out of Kentucky. Harrison and Tilman remained in Dizney all their lives.

When Ben became unable to live by himself, Harrison offered to let him live with his family, if Grandpa Ben deeded all his land over to him.

After some time Tilman discovered that Harrison was letting their father live in a building separate from his home. Harrison had a line strung from the building to his house so that Ben could come to the house by himself. Tilman didn't like this arrangement and took his father to his home where he spent the rest of his life. Harrison refused to deed back the land to Tilman, who was taking care of Ben. Harrison and Tilman never spoke again.

Martha passed away before Ben. Ben lived to be in his 90s. He was blind in his old age. Tilman died with Leukemia and Black Lung when he was 72. Since Grandpa Ben lived to a ripe old age of 90, he was probably not the carrier. Martha Shoemaker most probably was the carrier of this gene. Tilman's first born son also died from this Leukemia gene.

18

Benjamin Franklin Cloud Appeal

This is written word for word from transcripts taken from the original court records. I am not attempting to copyright this information only include it for informational purposes.

Court of Appeals of Kentucky

BEN CLOUD
v.
COMMONWEALTH OF KENTUCKY
May 1, 1886

Under an indictment for murder the admissions of other persons that they did the killing are not evidence; and equally is this true as to threats by other persons as to who did the killing.

*1 APPEAL FROM HARLAN CIRCUIT COURT.

OPINION BY JUDGE HOLT:

At a time not definitely fixed by the testimony, I saw that it was between noon and three o'clock of April 30, 1884, John Napier, while at work in a field, was without warning, so the evidence discloses, was shot and killed. There can be no question as to the guilt of persons who thus took human life. The appellant, Ben Cloud, together with nine other persons, was charged with the deed, the indictment charging a conspiracy among them to do the killing; and he, having obtained a separate trial, now seeks by this appeal to reverse a life sentence. It appears that the deceased and the defendants were neighbors; and from some cause not shown in the record they had become hostile to each other. Upon the day prior to the killing, several of the Napiers were at the house of a just ice of the neighborhood to attend an examining trial of the deceased upon the charge of burning the appellant's house. The defendants were also there, all of them being armed. The testimony shows that they were then acting in concert, and evidently each party was expecting and ready for a collision. The parties finally separated, however, without having any open difficulty, and the next day the deceased, while earning his bread by the sweat of his face, was shot by a person or persons upon the hill above where he was at work.

Two brothers of the deceased and the wife of one of them were at work with him, but in other parts of the field. One brother testifies that he saw the appellant and two other of the defendants in the field with guns and started to go to his brother; but one of them pointed his gun at him, while the other two went towards the deceased; and they being between him and the deceased, he turned and ran in the opposite direction. The other brother and his wife testify that when they heard the firing the ran to or near the place where the deceased had been at work, and saw the appellant and two of the defendants upon the hill above, but going away. Another witness says that he saw the same parties a short time before the killing with a fourth of a mile of the place where it occurred and going in that direction. They were seen by other parties about ten or eleven o'clock in the afternoon; and then went in the direction where the killing took place. All of these witnesses say that, when the appellant and the other two defendants were thus seen, they or at least some of them had guns.

The defense of the appellant was an alibi. He did not offer to introduce any of his co-defendants as witnesses; but to establish it relied upon the evidence of his sister-in-law and a sister of Richmond Pace. Who was also indicted with him and who, as some of the witnesses for the commonwealth say, was one of the three men along when the killing occurred. The first testifies that these three men were at Morgan Wynn's which is about a mile and a half from the scene of the killing, from, as she supposes, noon until three o'clock in the afternoon of the day of the killing, engaged in log rolling. The exact time of the tragedy, however, is not fixed by the witnesses. The other testifies that the three defendants whom the witnesses for the state say were present at the killing were upon that day at work at the log rolling. It is needless to review the testimony further in order to consider the questions now presented. The whole law of the case was given to the jury. No question of self-defense or manslaughter was presented. The accused relied upon an alibi. If true, then, it was impossible that the deceased could have been provoking his passion or endangering his life.

**2 The appellant proposed to prove that a man living in Virginia had, shortly before the killing, said that he intended to kill deceased. The ruling of the court in rejecting this proof was proper. On an indictment for murder the admissions of other persons that they did the killing are not evidenced, and equally is this true as to threats by other persons to do it. Wharton's Crim. Evid., 224; People v Murphy It is urged, however, that certain statements made by other of the defendants, when not in the presence of the appellant, were incompetent. Thus the state was allowed to prove by one witness that the defendan6t, Richmond Pace, said about two weeks before the killing that "John Napier had better watch or he would get his head busted", by another, that the defendant, Ben Wynn, said on the day the deceased was killed that "John Napier would be seen by some man at every point that day"; by another that the defendant, Green Cloud, had said (when does not appear) that "John Napier had thrown a rock at him and if he did it any more he would kill the Goddamn Indian"; by another, that some time after the killing, he ask the defendant, Acles Wynn, if when he heard the firing he saw any one, and that he replied: "Yes, I saw Richmond Pace run from of the ridge."

The lower court was probably of the opinion that a conspiracy to kill the deceased had been shown and therefore admitted these statements. It is, however unnecessary to determine this question. Clearly what Richmond Pace may have said was competent testimony, because the Commonwealth witnesses had already testified that he and the appellant were two of the three men engaged in the killing. It was so admissible upon the part of the state to show that the deceased had been arrested upon the charge of burning the house of the accused and that the latter was prosecuting the charge, as bearing upon the question of ill feeling between them or incentive to injure each other. The statement of Acles Wynn was undoubtedly incompetent. Admitting that a conspiracy to kill the deceased had been proved, yet it was not made until after the killing, and the declaration of a coconspirator is not competent after the aim of the conspiracy has been accomplished. In our opinion, however, formed after a careful examination of the record, the substantial rights of the appellant were not prejudiced by its introduction, nor by the testimony relating to what had been said by Wright and Ben Wynn and Green Cloud. The statements of the last three named persons in no way related to the appellant, and could not to any extent whatever have influenced the jury to believe that the accused was guilty.

Judgment affirmed

Jas. D. Black, J.H. Tinsly, for appellant

P.W. Hardin, J.M. Uthank, for Appellee

Ky.app.1886

BEN CLOUD v. COMMONWEALTH

13 Ky.Op. 1092, 7 Ky.L.Rptr. 818, 1886 WL 4037 (Ky)

END OF DOCUMENT

19

Affidavit swearing to the innocence of Benjamin F. Cloud and Richard Pace in the death John Napier

This is written word for word from transcripts taken from the original court records. I am not attempting to copyright this information only include it for informational purposes.

STATE OF KENTUCKY:
COUNTY OF FRANKLIN:
In the matter of:
Commonwealth of Kentucky:
     Vs   From Harlan County Criminal Court
Benjamin F. Cloud and:
Richard Pace: Defendants

AFFIDAVIT

The affiant herein, A. J. Napier, a prisoner in the Kentucky Penitentiary at Frankfort, Kentucky under judgment of the Harlan County Circuit Court for the term of One year for obtaining property under false pretense, says he is 32 years of age and was formerly a citizen of Harlan County, Kentucky. He is well acquainted with the above mentioned Benjamin F. Cloud and Richard Pace, now confined in the Kentucky Penitentiary at Frankfort, Kentucky for murder under judgment of the Harlan County Circuit Court (the alleged offense being the killing of one John Napier, brother of affidavit.

Affidavit says he has known the said Cloud and Pace from childhood. He says he has full information concerning all material matter of fact entering into the prosecution of said parties, Cloud and Pace aforesaid resulting in their conviction herein. The affiant says he used all the means in his power to secure the conviction of the said Cloud and Pace, that he obtained the temporary appointment of Deputy Sheriff of Harlan County for the purpose of prosecution of said parties herein named and used every opportunity offered by his office to secure the indictment and conviction of Cloud and Pace. He says he got and procured all parties available to appear and swear and testify to the best advantage against the accused Cloud and Pace, and that much admitted in evidence he knows to have been raise and perjured. He says the more swift the witness the more readily the affiant secured his attendance to testify. He says other of his affiant's family also joined to use every effort to compass the conviction of Cloud and Pace, and affiant states that he does not believe they were very particular in method of procuring and securing witnesses or of making testimony to reach the end in view. As to the innocence or guilt of accused affiant cannot state but says that he coached his affiants wife as to her testimony and that his affiant's brother, Fielding Napier acknowledged to affiant after the conviction of Cloud and Pace, that he the said Fielding Napier had sworn falsely in the said trial

The affiant says this statement is made without hope of reward or fear of punishment and only that the truth may be known and to relieve affiant's conscience of acts above written as far as herein possible and further he does not say.

—A.J. Napier

Subscribed and sworn to before me this 30th day of August 1892(cannot read last two digits).

—B.K. Ray

20

Divorce Court records of Benjamin F. and Judith Wynn Cloud

This is written word for word from transcripts taken from the original court records. I am not attempting to copyright this information only include it for informational purposes.

HARLAN CIRCUIT COURT

Petition in Equity

BENJAMIN F. CLOUD, JR., Plaintiff
AGAINST
JUDA CLOUD, Defendant

The plaintiff Benjamin F. Cloud, Jr. states, that he and defendant Judah Cloud were married to each other in Harlan County, Kentucky in the month of November 1876 and lived together as man and wife until the month of November 1885, when they separated. The separation occurred in Harlan County, Kentucky, also says the cause of divorce occurred in Harlan County, Kentucky and more than five years prior to the institution of this Suit.

Plaintiff states, that whilst plaintiff and Defendant lived together as man and wife the resided in Harlan County, Kentucky and separated in Harlan County, Kentucky and Plaintiff and Defendant both now reside in Harlan County, Kentucky and has so continuously resided for more than one year last past and for more than twelve months prior to the institution of this suit.

Plaintiff states that since the separation of Plaintiff and Defendant in November 1885, they have neither lived, slept or cohabitated together.

Plaintiff states that since the separation of Plaintiff and defendant, that Defendant has been guilty of lewd and lascivious conduct, that Defendant has been guilty of committing adultery at _____. times and places with Ransom Middleton, Benjamin F. Fields, Ed Jones, John King and Walter Middleton (Carr's son) and others in Harlan County Kentucky.

Wherefore Plaintiff prays for a divorce from the bonds of matrimony, and to be released to all the rights and privileges of a married man, and for all proper relief, this June 25, 1897.

—George B. Turner, Attorney for Plaintiff

21

Deposition of John Thomas

This is written word for word from transcripts taken from the original court records. I am not attempting to copyright this information only include it for informational purposes.

Taken on the 19th day of July 1897 in the law office of DH Smith in the Town of Mount Pleasant, Harlan County, Ky to be read as evidence in an action between Benjamin F. Cloud, Plaintiff and Judah Cloud, Defendant, pending in the Harlan Circuit Court. The witness after first being duly sworn states:

Question: State your age, occupation and residence, are you acquainted with the parties to the suit?
Answer: I am 21 years of age a farmer by occupation. I reside on Yokum Creek in Harlan County, Kentucky. I am acquainted with the parties to this suit.
Question: Are they or not married to each other, and if so state when and where they were married?
Answer: My understanding is they are married to each other. They were married to each other in Harlan County, Kentucky as far back as I can recollect.
Question: State whether or not they are now living together as man and wife, or are they separated and apart.
Answer: They are now living separate and apart.
Question: State when and where the separation occurred.
Answer: The separation occurred here about eleven years ago in Harlan County, Kentucky.
Question: State all you may know in regard to the separation.

Answer: Plaintiff was convicted to the penitentiary for his life for the killing of John Napier in about the year of 1885, since which time they have been separate and apart. The cause of divorce occurred in Harlan County, Kentucky more than five years prior to the institution of this suit. They each separated in Harlan County, Kentucky where the separation occurred and had so continuously resided for more than one year prior to its institution of the suit and now both reside in Harlan County, Kentucky. They have neither lived, slept nor cohabitated together since the separation in the year 1885 so far as I know and believe.

Question: State whether or not you know of Defendant, Judah Cloud being guilty of lewd and luscious conduct since the separation occurred between her and B. F. Cloud, Jr., Plaintiff and if so, where?

Answer: I have it occurred in Harlan County, Kentucky.

Question: You will please state whether or not since the marriage of Plaintiff and Defendant, you know of Defendant being guilty of adultery and if so, you will state when, where, how often and with who committed.

Answer: I know of Defendant since her marriage with Plaintiff being guilty of adultery about the year 1885 and on up to the present time in Harlan County, Kentucky on Yokums Creek. I can not state how often but I know of her committing adultery at various times and places with myself and William Middleton (Carr's son), Ed Jones and Sam Middleton

And further this defendant sayeth with his mark X (John Thomas)

Also the deposition of John King taken at the same time and place and for the cause stated in the caption.

22

Deposition of John King

This is written word for word from transcripts taken from the original court records. I am not attempting to copyright this information only include it for informational purposes.

Taken on the 19th day of July 1897 in the law office of DH Smith in the Town of Mount Pleasant, Harlan County, Ky to be read as evidence in an action between Benjamin F. Cloud, Plaintiff and Judah Cloud, Defendant, pending in the Harlan Circuit Court. The witness after first being duly sworn states:

Question: State your age, residence and occupation, and your acquaintance with the Plaintiff Benjamin F. Cloud, Jr. and Judah Cloud.
Answer: I am 40 years of age. I reside on Jones' Creek in Harlan County, Kentucky. I am a farmer by occupation. I am acquainted with the Plaintiff and Defendant in this action.
Question: Are or not Plaintiff and Defendant married to each other, and if so when and where were they married?
Answer: My understanding is that they were married to each other in Harlan County, Kentucky about the year 1876.
Question: Are they now living together as man and wife, or are they living separate and apart?
Answer: They are now living separate and apart.
Question: You will please state when and where the separation occurred and all you may know about it.
Answer: They separated in Harlan County, Kentucky in about the year 1885. About this time the Plaintiff and Benjamin F. Cloud was convicted and sent to the penitentiary for his killing of John Napier. The separation and cause of divorce occurred in Harlan County, Kentucky more than five

years prior to the institution of this suit. Whilst Plaintiff and Defendant lived together as man and wife they resided in Harlan County, Kentucky and Separated in Harlan County, Kentucky. Plaintiff and Defendant both now reside in Harlan County, Kentucky and has so continuously resided for more than one year last past and for more than twelve months prior to the institution of this suit. Plaintiff and Defendant have neither lived, slept or cohabited together since the separation, so far as I know or believe.

Question: State whether or not you know of Defendant being guilty of Adultery since the separation in 1885 and if so, you will state when and where it occurred, how often, and with whom committed.

Answer: I do know of Defendant committing adultery since the separation. On Jones' creek in Harlan County, Kentucky about the year of 1895 whilst Plaintiff was in the Penitentiary and prior to his being pardoned out of the Penitentiary by the Governor of Kentucky. I know of Defendant committing adultery twice with myself.

Question: State, whether or not Defendant had a child and heir whilst Plaintiff was confined in the Penitentiary, if so, how long prior to his being pardoned out by the Governor, and if you ever had any conversation with the Defendant in regard to her having the child, you will please state who she said was the father, when and where the conversation occurred, who was present and all she said in said conversation.

Answer: My understanding is that she did have a child whilst Plaintiff was in prison some two or three years after Plaintiff was convicted and imprisoned and some seven or eight years prior to his being pardoned by the Governor. I had a conversation with Defendant in regard to this child in which she said Ransom Middleton was the father of the child. The conversation occurred on Jones Creek in Harlan County, Kentucky some two or three years ago. I do not remember whether any one was present of not. She said in that conversation that Ransom Middleton would not do any thing for the child and that she never would fool with him any more.

And further this deponent sayeth now JOHN KING

23

Archibald Presley and Emily Brewer Presley

Archibald Presley was born in Tennessee in 1845 and died about 1912 in Virginia. Archie was the son of Martin Presley and Rachel (unknown) Presley. Archibald was married three times. His second wife was Emily Brewer, daughter of Sylvaneous Brewer and Amelia Moore; they both had to be full blood Cherokee Indian because Emily Brewer was considered to be a full blood Cherokee Indian. Archie and Emily's children were considered to be half Cherokee Indian.

Archie and Emily Presley migrated from Hawkins County, Tennessee during the winter of 1880 or 1881. The family crossed the frozen Clinch River into Virginia. All of their possessions were loaded into a wagon which was driven by Archie. Emily walked across the frozen river carrying Andy who was around 2 years old and Emily who was a few months old. The circumstances of the journey to Virginia were not known. The best time to make a journey of this kind would have been when the river was not frozen. There were numerous ferries to cross most rivers with wagon and horses at this time.

By 1885 Archie and Emily Presley were living in Harlan County, Kentucky. They ended up in Dizney, Kentucky.

The children of Archibald and Emily Brewer Presley were:
1) Andrew Jackson Presley was born in Tennessee on October 9, 1878 and died June 12, 1924 in Harlan County, Ky. He married Drucilla Hall on October 4, 1901 in Harlan County, Ky. Drucilla was the daughter of Carlo Brittain Hall and Julia Ann Lankford

2) Millie Presley was born in Tennessee on September?, 1880 and died on June 12, 1924 in Harlan County, Ky. She married Samuel Thomas on May 27, 1894 in Harlan County, Ky. Samuel was the son of Henry Thomas and Delia Turner.

3. Paralee Presley was born August 17, 1885 in Harlan County, Ky. She died November 24, 1974 in Harlan County, Ky. Paralee was married to William Middleton on September 2, 1899 in Harlan County, Kentucky

4. Jesse James Presley, born August 14, 1887 in Harlan County, Ky. And died on March 24, 1959 in Harlan County, Ky. He married Elizabeth Wynn on March 21, 1907 in Harlan County. Elizabeth was the daughter of James Wynn and Nancy Shoemaker.

5. Rachel Presley born on September 26, 1889 in Harlan County, Ky and died on January 26, 1961 in Harlan County, Kentucky. Rachel married Isaac Madden on March 17, 1906 in Harlan County, Ky.

6. Green Presley born on October 14, 1893 in Harlan County, Ky and died on July 7, 1926 in Harlan County, Kentucky. Green married Eva Mae Durham on March 15, 1920 in Harlan County, Ky. She was the daughter of Clarence Durham and Maggie Grady.

In the 1950s Witt Presley and his son Amos, who was a preacher, came to Dizney to hold a revival at the Locust Grove Baptist Church. The name Presley was not a common name in Harlan County. The Presley family in Dizney began asking the preacher and his father if they were kin to Archie Presley and Emily Brewer Presley.

To the surprise of all of the Presley family members of Dizney, Witt just happened to be one of the brothers of Archie. None of Archie's Tennessee relatives had seen or heard from him and his family since the winter of 1880.

There was a barn raising in Tennessee. Archie played the fiddle at the celebration after they finished building the barn. Archie left the dance before it was over and went home to get his wife and two children. They were never seen again. No one ever knew what had happened at the dance to cause Archie to take his family and leave his family forever.

Witt recounted the family ancestry for his new found relatives. Archie and Emily never spoke about their family. The only reason I can think of that a person would just disappear would be if his life or his family's life was threatened. Witt must have been very happy to go home and tell them that he had finally found out what had happened to Archibald and Emily Brewer Presley.

24

Andrew Jackson and Drucilla Hall Presley

Andrew Jackson Presley was born on October 9, 1878 in Hawkins County, Tennessee. Andy died June 12, 1924 in Dizney, Kentucky of Tuberculosis. His parents were Archibald Presley and Hannah Emily Brewer. Hannah Emily Brewer was the daughter of Sylvaneous Brewer and Amelia Moore. Amelia Moore was a full blooded Cherokee Indian. Drucilla Hall Presley was born 1882 in Elcomb, Harlan County Kentucky and died in 1962 in Dizney, Kentucky. The parents of Drucilla were Carlo Brittain Hall and Julia Ann Lankford. Andrew and Drucilla were married on October 4, 1901.

Andrew Jackson Presley was a blacksmith, farmer and sometimes bounty hunter. Andy had lived in the mountains of Dizney Kentucky since about 1882. His family came from Hawkins County, Tennessee in the winter of 1880/1881. Sometimes the county Sheriff would call upon Andy to help them catch a fugitive, especially if the fugitive was in the area where the Presley family lived. Andy was part Cherokee Indian and a very good tracker. If Andy had caught a fugitive and it was too late to travel to Harlan he would bring the fugitive home and tie him to his bedpost and go to sleep. At day light he would take the fugitive to Harlan and claim his payment.

The children of Andy and Drucilla Presley were:

(1) Leona Presley was born July 5, 1902 and died October 2, 1988 in Harlan, Kentucky. She first met Bill Turner and married Tilman Thomas Cloud in October 1924 in Harlan County, Kentucky. Tilman was the son of Benjamin Franklin Cloud and Martha Shoemaker Cloud.

(2) Elmer Farley Presley was born on August 24, 1904, and died November 24, 1977, in Harlan, Kentucky. He married Maudie Marie Durham on April 16, 1927, in Harlan County, Kentucky. Maudie was the daughter of Clarence Durham and Maggie Grady Durham.

(3) Robert Lee Presley was born on March 20, 1907 and died on September 1, 1967 of a heart attack in Salt Lake City, Utah. Robert was married to Vilda Skinner Harris.

(4) Cecil Skidmore Presley was born on September 12, 1909 and died on January 26, 1968 of a heart attack in Lexington, Kentucky. Cecil was married to Nettie Napier on May 9, 1936 in Harlan County, Kentucky.

(5) Johnnie Gilbert Presley was born October 5, 1912 and died on October 4,1955 in Somerset, Kentucky. Johnnie was married to Ruth Absher on April 21, 1934 in Harlan County, Ky.

(6) Golda Presley was born on April 25, 1915 and died on January 10, 1966 in Dayton, Ohio. Golda married (1) Worley Adams on October 18, 1940 and (2) Howard Stubblefield.

(7) Clyde Green Presley was born on April 11, 1917 and died on August 19, 1979 in Louisville, Kentucky. Clyde married Minnie Brewer on April 28, 1937 in Harlan County, Kentucky.

(8) Stella Myrtle Presley was born on July 30, 1918 and died September 11, 1976 in Cincinnati, Ohio. Stella married Lloyd Freeman on November 16, 1937 in Harlan County, Kentucky.

(9) Clark Hall Presley was born on July 16, 1920 and died on November 6, 1960 in Tennessee. Clark married Sarah Emmaline Stoner on August 12, 1941, in Harlan County, Kentucky.

Drucilla and Andy are buried in the cemetery behind the Church of God in Bills Creek, Dizney, Kentucky.

A few years after Andy died Drucilla remarried W. M. Lawson. Mr. Lawson did not get along with Grandma Presley's children and left her after about five years of marriage. Grandma refused to leave her home and follow him. He divorced her. Grandma Presley lived in the bottom land near the highway in the middle of Dizney. This land was in the valley that was surrounded by the four hollers.

My mother would take me with her when she went to Grandma Presley's house. Mom would give her a sponge-bath or wash her hair or to help around the house. I am not sure if this was a weekly thing or if Pauline Grubbs (daddy's sister) helped out also.

I would go with mom whenever she went out of the holler. I loved to watch mom comb grandma's hair and roll it into a bun on top of her head and put the old fashion hair pins in to secure it. Grandma had the most beautiful yellow hair.

Grandma used to fuss at me for chewing bubble gum. "It will rot your teeth out", she would say to me. She was so right. I have been paying for that bubblegum all these years.

Mom and I would walk out of the holler past Aunt Pauline's house on the right where the holler ended. Before crossing the Big Bridge we turn onto a dirt wagon path to the right of the bridge. The path was at the edge of Yokum creek that ran through our town. We walked passed about four small houses, on the right, that were set back at the foot of the mountain. At the end of this dirt road mom opened a gate that was attached to a fence that ran to the right all the way to the foot of the mountain. Grandma Presley's land began here. There was a big corn field that we passed in the summer, before we got to the path that led to Grandma Presley's house.

At the end of that field there was a small bridge to the left that lead to the road on the other side of Yokum creek. To the right of the bridge was a short foot path that opened up into Grandma's front yard. Her land was two or three acres

There was nothing in the middle of the yard but weeds and a few sun-flowers flowers. The cornfield surrounded the yard. I mostly remember the sunflowers. I have lots of sunflowers in my yard each summer because they remind me of her and I love them. Her house was built close to the mountain. There was a porch across the front of the house with wide steps leading up to the porch.

On the porch there was always a couple of cane bottom chairs to sit and take a rest in. There was a door with an outside screen door in the middle of the house with a window on either side. Opening the front door and enter-ing the living room you will see to your left a tall radio cabinet. The cabinet was about three and a half feet tall and two feet wide. In the front a few inches from the top was a tiny radio face with vertical lines and numbers. Just below were some tiny round knobs for turning the radio on and scrolling through the stations. Sometime when my cousin Sheila and I slept over, Grandma Presley would find a station and let us listen to the radio. This was in the mid 1950s.

There were no doors inside of the house. To the right of the front door was a doorway leading into grandma's bedroom. In the wall separating the living room and the bedroom was a two sided fireplace. You could build a fire in either room and the smoke would go up the same chimney.

The bed was in the middle of the room with the headboard touching the outside wall. At each corner of the bed were tall round posts. The purpose I guess was to hang your clothes when you went to bed. The furniture was very old. I only remember a bed and a shiffrobe. There were no closets so the shiffrobe held all the clothes and linens.

Walking towards the back of the house from their bedroom was another smaller bed room. I just cannot imagine five or more children sleeping in this one small room. This is where Sheila and I slept when we slept overnight.

Turning left you entered the doorway to the Kitchen. Against the wall dividing the kitchen and living room was an old fashion cupboard. It was not too different from today's china cabinets. At the top there were doors that had grey tin metal with wood only on the edges of the doors. There was a picture in the tin made by punching tiny holes in the metal.

There was a rectangle shaped wood table with four cane bottom chairs in the middle of the kitchen. The back wall of the kitchen facing the mountain had a dry sink with either a cabinet around it or a cloth skirt. Above the sink was a window that looked out to the mountain.

To the left of the sink was an old fashion wood cooking stove against the side wall near the door leading outside.

In the side yard was a pump for water. Behind grandma's house was a small building used to store tools and whatever else that could not be stored in the house. A few feet away from this building was the outside toilet.

Sheila and I would sleep over in the summer when there was no school or on the weekends. We slept in the extra bedroom. I would lay awake looking out the window at the stars in the sky. I remember seeing a shooting star flash across the night sky. Sheila and I would lay awake whispering and sharing secrets. Sometimes we slept in the living room on a folding bed, with a nice roaring fire going in the fireplace. We watched the fire and the shadows it cast on the ceiling and were lulled into a peaceful sleep.

Grandma would make us breakfast. This was a treat for me because I usually had oatmeal, pancakes or eggs, gravy and biscuits. She made a bowl of rice and toasted bread in her oven. She would put sugar into the rice and set a plate of it in front of us. The rice would be spooned on top of the bread and eaten. That is one of the comfort foods I never got enough of as I grew into an adult. I wanted my girls to experience the same comforting feeling so I made them rice with toast too. I usually made this meal for breakfast or whenever they did not feel good.

Grandma also introduced me and mom to another dish that she was fond of. She would put cottage cheese in a bowl and empty peaches over it and add a little mayonnaise. I still eat that too.

On the right side of grandma's house was a foot path that led up the hill to a house where her son Clyde and his family lived. They were close enough to walk to grandma's house and check on her. Clyde's children did chores for grandma.

Andrew - Drusilla
Leona - Elmer
Presley - Taken 1905

Kim Jones Dean

ANDREW JACKSON & DRUCILLA HALL PRESLEY
LEONA & ELMER PRESLEY

DRUCILLA HALL PRESLEY FAMILY
1st Row: Larry, Stella, Drucilla, Leona, Goldie
Lloyd Freeman, Clark, Johnny, Elmer, Vilda, Robert and Lola
On Porch are all grandchildren

JESSIE JAMES & ELIZABETH WYNN PRESLEY
CARLOS, GREEN, MINNIE & MAE

25

Petition in Equity of W. H. Lawson

This is written word for word from transcripts taken from the original court records. I am not attempting to copyright this information only include it for informational purposes.

W.N. Lawson, Plaintiff

Vs

Drucilla P. Lawson

The plaintiff W. N. Lawson, states that he and the defendant Drucilla P. Lawson, were married in this State in the year of 1927, and they each now reside and have continuously resided in Harlan County, Kentucky, for more than one year next before the commencement of this action; that the cause of divorce hereinafter set out, occurred in this State, and within five years next before the commencement of this action.

The plaintiff states that he and the defendant lived together as man and wife from their marriage until on or about December 15th, 1932, at which time defendant, without any fault or like fault on his part, abandoned his home and refuses to and has not since said time lived or cohabitated with the defendant; that during the time they lived together he always treated the defendant in a kind and affectionate manner and provided comfortably for her support.

The plaintiff states that at the time he and the defendant were married as aforesaid, he had children by a former marriage and that the defendant had children by a former marriage, that he went into the home of the defendant to reside and did reside therein until the above alleged separation and until such time the home became disorganized by the continuous disagreements among the members of said families, and by reason thereof the plaintiff departed there from and went to and did arrange to obtain or rent another house in which to live near his work and did thereafter go to the defendant and invite, prevail on and offer her to come into his house and live. Wherein they could reside in peace and harmony to themselves, but the defendant failed and refused so to do; the defendant by her conduct, demeanor and attitude produced the intolerable condition which forced the plaintiff to withdraw from the joint habitation to a more peaceful and less disturbing one, all of which was without fault or like fault on his part, and he caused a continued separation without cohabitation each with the other for more than one year before the commencement of this action, and the defendant has since formed a devout determination which she has expressed never to live with or have any further relations with the plaintiff as husband and wife.

WHEREFORE the plaintiff prays the judgment of the court divorcing he and the defendant absolutely from the bonds of matrimony, and for all equitable relief to which he is justly entitled.

—Gus B. Bruner,
Attorney for the Plaintiff

The affiant W. N. Lawson, says that he is the plaintiff in this action, that he has read the statements and allegations of the foregoing petition which are true and correct.

—W. N Lawson

Subscribed and sworn to before me by W. H. Lawson, this 25th day of July, 1934

—Gus B. Bruner, Notary Public
Harlan County, Kentucky

26

Letter to W. H. Lawson from Drucilla Presley Lawson

This is written word for word from transcripts taken from the original court records. I am not attempting to copyright this information only include it for informational purposes.

Mr. Lawson, I don't see why you thought I was so angry. I treated you my very best. I could and for as asking you to stay longer on Sunday I couldn't afford to do that, because we are separated for good. It isn't worth while for us to try to live together and you such a distaste against my children. You ought to have known before you left that I couldn't forsake my children and you told me time and again that you didn't want a one of them about you and you were always telling me you didn't intend for them to eat up what you worked out and I am thankful today that I can say and tell the truth that I never spoke an unnecessary word to you about one of your children in my life or you either. You know I always treated you and them kind in every respect, but as far as me being unkind, I think my credit will stand before man and before the almighty God at the day of Judgment. God knows I wish you and all your children well. Yes I remember 5 years ago and all a long between them and now. You know that we have nearly worn out everything I had on the place and nothing new coming and what is it worth our while to try to stay together any longer so I hope while I can remember so much all a long I hope you can remember one year ago so I haven't forgot anything. Myself I only look to God in all things and I expect to trust him as long as breath holds mind and body together. But remember I haven't forgot anything but I can let things pass by easy as possible for I have more worry than I am able to bear but thanks be to the Blessed Lord the time will soon come that all my troubles and sorrows will be over so I hope you want get any further disgusted than you already are. May joy, peace and happiness dwell with you forever. You have a chance now to help your children and may be while. My children has no one to depend on they can make their own living so this is all I know to say.

—Drucilla Presley

27

W. H. Lawson Granted Divorce Decree

This is written word for word from transcripts taken from the original court records. I am not attempting to copyright this information only include it for informational purposes.

W. N. Lawson,
Plaintiff

Vs.

Drucilla P. Lawson
Defendant

This action having been submitted to the court up on the pleadings, depositions and exhibits, and the court being sufficiently advised, it is considered and adjudged by the court that the plaintiff W. N. Lawson, be and he is hereby divorced from the bonds of matrimony with the defendant Drucilla P. Lawson, and restores to all of the rights and privileges of an unmarried man.

It is further ordered and adjudged by the court that the plaintiff pay the cost of this action, and this case is now stricken from the courts docket.

28

Dizney Men Die in Gunfight

Green Presley and Joe Thomas decided to settle their differences with guns. Presley shot Thomas a number of times and Thomas died almost immediately. Thomas was able to get off one shot during the gun fight and that one shot would prove to be fatal to Mr. Presley in the early morning hours following the fight.

Green Presley was a brother to Andrew Jackson Presley who was the husband of Drucilla Hall Presley. Green Presley was married to Elizabeth Wynn Presley.

An inquest was held the following morning and as a result Robert Presley and Elmer Presley (Children of Andrew and Drucilla Presley) were arrested and jailed. Thomas supposedly made a statement before he died that Robert and Elmer Presley were involved in the gun fight. A witness testified to Mr. Thomas's comments.

At the inquest George Madden claimed to be present at the scene of the gun fight and according to him, Green Presley was in a quarrel with Dewey Hensley. His two nephews were also present. Joe Thomas came to the scene of the quarrel and attempted to resolve the fight between the two men.

Green Presley stopped arguing with Mr. Hensley and turned his anger on Joe Thomas. Thomas turned and began to run away from the three Presley men. Thomas fell and the three Presley men began to beat him.

Elmer Presley was supposed to have handed a pistol to Green Presley and Green shot Thomas several times. Thomas was able to get off one shot that struck Green Presley.

There was other testimony that Thomas shot Green Presley first and he took the gun that Elmer Presley was holding and fired at Thomas several times. Both Thomas and Presley leave a widow and three children.

In speaking with Elmer's daughter (Helen) I was told that the out come was that neither Elmer nor Robert Presley were charged with having anything to do with this crime. Elmer and Robert are my great Uncles, as their mother Drucilla Hall Presley is my great grandmother. Elmer and his family lived all their lives in Stretchneck holler just below my house.

29

Tilman Thomas Cloud

Tilman Thomas Cloud, son of Benjamin Franklin Cloud and Martha Shoemaker, grandson of Ben Frank Cloud and Nancy Middleton. Tilman Cloud, Jr. is my father.

Ben Cloud was a blacksmith by trade. He was born in Tennessee but moved to Harlan County when Tilman was a small child. Ben Cloud bought land in what was known as Jones Creek on top of the mountain. They were dirt poor. Tilman Cloud was born 1/23/1901. His siblings were Josephine born 1898, Ida born 1/28/1903, Harrison Cloud born 11/14/1904, Matilda born 9/22/1906, Alberta born 11/28/1908, Doxie born 7/16/1914 and Octavia born 4/11/1917.

Tilman Cloud was a coal miner, a beekeeper, blacksmith, and farmer. He had chickens and roosters. There was a red rooster that was so mean that he would chase you if you came near the house and jump at you and hit you with his sharp spurs. He always had a cow for milk and butter. He fed his family by gathering food from the surrounding mountains, such as apples, pears, walnuts, beach nuts and vegetables from his garden. There were grape vines on the hill behind the back of the house above the rock wall. Papow took care of the grape vines.

Behind the house the dirt had been dug back two or three feet and a rock wall was built to about two and a half. This was to hold back the dirt wall upon which the grape fines were planted. There was a wooden frame built which the grapes would climb. They would be large deep purple sour grapes. Mamaw would make grape jelly out of them. They also were perfect grapes for home made wine.

Papaw Cloud worked in the mines all his life. He never owned a car. He would either take the bus from Jones Store or start walking and someone would pick him up before he got to Evarts. In Evarts he would either get a haircut or buy some groceries. He usually got a taxi to bring him home.

In the late 50s Papaw Cloud retired because he became sick with Leukemia and Black Lung.

I never got close to Papaw Cloud. To me he was a grouchy old man. He liked to grab me and scratch my face with his whiskers. He was not a person who ever showed any physical emotions of love, hugging, or kissing. He and Mamaw used to argue with each other. Not loud yelling, just picking at each other, kind of like a boxing match one would get in a jab and the other would reply in kind.

Papaw Cloud usually did most of the physical work around the house. He milked the cows, took care of the garden, his bees.

There was a constant battle keeping the weeds, trees, and brush from overtaking everything. There were no lawnmowers or weed eaters. A sickle was used. This was a long handled tool with a sharp curved blade at the end. People used that to cut the grasses and small trees. Papaw would walk around the hills around his property carrying a potato sack filled with rocks and dirt. He would light the underbrush and let it burn, but before it got out of control he would smother it with the sack of rock and dirt.

I used to wonder where Papaw Cloud got this idea to burn the underbrush. I was reading about Jamestown, Virginia and learned that the local Indians used this method to keep their land clear. Those Indian people also knew the importance of rotating their crops.

Every summer relatives of my family would come in to visit. That would be a great time. There would be lots of food and deserts at their house for everyone. Their house was pretty big and there were enough beds for the visitors or they would take turns sleeping at relatives houses. This would be one time that daddy would let us spend as much time at their house.

Usually Daddy did not want us going there too much. Guess he thought we would bother them or mooch food from them, which we did. Whenever we came home from Louisville for a visit we always stayed with them.

Papaw bought a TV before anyone else in the holler had one. They also had a bathroom built onto their house and a well dug. That was amazing to have an indoor bathroom and water (all of which we never had). Watching TV became a favorite past time of Papaw and Mamaw. But of course, Papaw was the boss of what was to be watched when he was around. He watched the news, television preachers and anything having to do with politics. He loved Harry Truman, didn't care too much for IKE. Also I remember a big crowd every now and then watching the Friday night fights. He also loved TV western.

Papow Cloud always had a few bee hives. I don't know if this is something he learned from his father or just wanted to give it a try. His bee hives were placed up on the side of the hill from the front yard. I imagine that was so that we grandchildren did not disturb them and get stung. When he decided to collect honey he would put on his bee suit. The suit was made out of very thin mesh wrapped around a cylinder that he would put over his head. He wore a type of cape that went around his shoulders.

He had a contraption that made smoke and the smoke was blown into the hives. The smoke would put the bees into a stupor so that the honey could be gathered. The honey combs were taken from the hive and put into a large round aluminum bowl. Honey was put into canning jars in the same manner of the fruit and vegetables. The vegetables had to be very hot to kill any bacteria before they were sealed into the glass jars. Honey was not heated. The honey could be stored for a few weeks and be as fresh as the first day it was taken from the bee hives.

Honey came in several different varieties depending upon which tree or bush the bee collected the nectar from. The different flavored and color honey depended on what season it was and which plants and trees were in bloom. When the hives were robbed for their honey the bees were very upset for about a week. They would sting anyone that came anywhere near Papaw's yard. Sometimes they flew as far as down the road to our house.

Finally they would settle down and begin to collect new nectar to make more honey.

After we moved to Louisville, Kentucky in 1960, I would come back every summer and spend about a month with them. Papaw died in 1972 of complications of Leukemia and Black Lung. My father Junior Cloud (Tilman, Jr.) also died from Leukemia in 2003.

It may have been a coincidence, but it seems that Papaw Cloud and my dad's symptoms got worse after their bee colony started to die.

TILMAN THOMAS CLOUD AND HALF SISTERS
NARCISSUS AND DELILIAH

30

Leona Presley Cloud

Leona Presley Cloud was born in Harlan County, Kentucky in 1902 and died in the fall of 1988. She married Tilman Thomas Cloud in 1924. Tilman Thomas Cloud, Jr. was born in 1925. Shortly after Junior's third birthday they moved from Brittains Creek, Kentucky to Dizney in Stretchneck Holler. They lived in a small cabin above what was to be their family homestead. In a year or so, Tilman bought the house below this small cabin and the surrounding land that went with the house. Their children after Junior were Lola, Asbury (Berry), Pauline and Lora.

Tilman never helped with the women's work. Mamaw Cloud had a lot of jobs such as taking care of the children, keeping the house clean, washing clothes, canning food, milking the cow, churning the milk for buttermilk and butter and of course cooking all the meals.

Leona worked as hard as any man. When the children were small Leona would put what ever she could sell from the garden into a burlap sack, throw it across her shoulder and walk from Dizney, following a trail directly over Bonnie Blue Mountain to the Coal Mines in Virginia to sell her vegetables. The coal company supplied transportation for their employees from Kentucky to get to the mines. If she was too late to get a ride at the top of Bonny Blue Mountain, she walked the rest of the way down the mountain to the coal mines. She also sold buttermilk and eggs to area families.

With the money she made she bought the children new shoes and coats at the Pace general store each year. Tilman never offered to buy these things for the kids. He probably knew she would come up with the money somehow.

Tilman worked hard and expected everyone to go to sleep at dusk as he did. I am sure this was a habit from growing up in the pioneer times, and not wanting to waste what candles and coal oil they had for their lamps. Mamaw Cloud would take the kids outside a good distance from the house to play when Papaw went to bed. When she thought Papaw was asleep she would very quietly return to the house and put the kids to bed.

I loved to spend time with Mamaw Cloud when mom and dad would let me. It was usually when mom was helping her with something. I have many happy memories of her kitchen.

When the cow got milked and the milk was brought to the kitchen, Mamaw Cloud would use a thin cloth to strain the milk. She was doing this to separate the thick cream from the milk. The cream was kept separate and used for coffee, and baking. She always saved extra milk to drink with meals. A portion of the milk would sit on the kitchen table in a very large aluminum pot or ceramic bowl until it thickened and smelled real sour.

She would bring her churn into the kitchen. After taking the dasher and top lid off she would pour the soured milk into the churn. The milk was part thick matter and some liquid. The dasher was a long round stick about an inch round that had two flat two inch pieces of wood nailed to the bottom of the round stick in the shape of an X. This was called the "dasher". The X shape helped to mix up the milk mixture until it turned to buttermilk and butter.

The small round lid with a hole in the center fit down through the round piece of wood and laid on top of the ceramic butter churn about one inch below the rim of the churn. The round lid had a hole in the middle with a small space around the wood dasher where the milk would splash onto it and you could see the tiny pieces of butter start to form. The butter milk had to be a certain thick consistency before Mamaw would say that the process was done.

When I was allowed to help churn, Mamaw would lay a dishcloth over my lap and scoot the churn up to the front of the cane bottom chair I was sitting on. I would churn until one arm got tired and then I would change to the other. It seemed like an awfully long time to make butter and butter-milk, but I never quit, I just rested when I was tired.

Leona would gather all the butter that was on top of the buttermilk in the churn put it into a bowl and pour cold water over it. She would beat the but-ter with a wooden spoon, changing the water for clean water until the water was clear and the butter was a bright yellow color and clung together in a tight round ball in the bowl.

Wax paper and the butter molds would be brought out. The molds were made out of wood. With the wooden spoon Mamaw would fill the round wooden butter mold. The round perfectly molded pound of butter with a pretty design from the bottom of the mold would be turned out on to the wax paper. Each pound would be covered completely with the wax paper and put in the refrigerator or freezer, when she had a newer refrigerator. This was in the middle 50s when I was between seven to eight years old.

Leona would make grape jelly from the juice and pulp of the grapes col-lected by Papaw Cloud from the back of the house. She took the juice, and added sugar and pectin. The juice would be heated on the stove until the sugar melted. She then put it into jars which were sealed with lids and round caps that screwed onto the top of the jars. This was the same type of jars that were used to can the garden vegetables. Not only the grape jelly tasted deli-cious but all the canned foods she made tasted good.

After the jar lids made a popping sound, sending the signal that they had sealed, they would be brought out the front door, down the front steps and around to the front of the house and placed into the block enclosed base-ment of the house where it was dry and cool.

I believe that Papaw got his grape vine roots from Andy Campaganri, a native of Verona, Italy who lived on top of the mountain in Dizney. He worked in the coal mines in Kenvir and Black Mountain for around 40 years. Andy had a big grape orchard and made home made wine in the fash-ion of his homeland on top of the mountain in Dizney where he lived.

He not only drank the wine he also sold it and probably bartered it for things he could not afford to pay cash money for. Bartering was a way of life for the people in this region of Kentucky.

I remember as a child walking down the road with mom, we were going to Milt Jones store, and along came Andy walking down the road with his beard down to his chest and overalls and boots on. Needless to say he frightened me a lot. I was not curious to find out who he was.

Leona was a talented baker. She could stir up the best tasting cornbread and biscuits ever. Apples and Pears were planted in the hills of Stretchneck holler by Tilman's father and uncles. They cross pollinated different apples to make new verities. Apples were a big staple in their diet. When the apples ripened they would be carried down from the mountains in burlap sacks by Papaw Cloud, dad and my brother Roger. A lot of people came up the holler on the way to the apple orchard to get apples. The trees were not owned by anyone. They were shared by all.

There were a lot of wild berries that grew near the creek banks such as blackberries, raspberries and strawberries. Rhubarb was a perennial fruit that came back every year and a great cobbler was made from it. All fruits and vegetables were canned so that there was food all year long.

There were different varieties of apples in the mountains of Dizney. The apples ripened at different times. There would be apples in the spring and fall. Mamaw and mom would never dream of wasting apples by letting them fall on the ground and rot, they always had to be picked so that applesauce could be made and canned. Cooked apples with sugar and cinnamon were eaten with biscuits for breakfast almost every morning.

The apples were washed, pealed and cooked on the coal and wood kitchen stove. The cooked apples were then put into canning jars and the lids and caps were screwed on tightly. The hot jars would be set on the kitchen table on a cloth until we heard the pop that announced the sealing process. This meant that the contents were sealed as tight as if they were processed professionally today. When it came time to open one of these jars it required a lot of strength to unscrew the lids.

A lot of those apples would be eaten by us as we pealed them. Mamaw Cloud loved her apples. Pies were made from certain kinds of apples. The apples had to be a very hard texture so that they would not turn to mush in the pie when during baking. The apples had to come out of the over in a firm texture with the homemade pie crust a golden brown. The pie pans were old and tarnished from baking pies for so many years.

Mamaw Cloud was known far and wide for her apple sauce stack cake. The only spice that was cheap enough for her to buy during the 20s and 30s was cinnamon. She used it as a flavoring in her cooked apples, pies and stack cake. The apples would be flavored with either molasses, or honey, when they could not afford to pay the price for sugar. The apples had lots of natural water in them so they needed to be cooked until all the water was boiled away and thick fine apples pieces were left. The apples were cooked in aluminum or a cast iron pot on the coal stove for hours. The applesauce would have a brown color to it when it was done.

Mamaw Cloud's famous applesauce cake was loved by all. The cake ingredients would be stirred up. The texture would resemble her biscuit. She would roll a portion into a ball and place it into the cast iron skillet. The dough would be flattened into the bottom of the skillet to make very skinny layers. The layers would be made and laid onto dishtowels on the table to cool.

The process of putting the cake together was very easy. The applesauce was put between the layers. Usually the cake would have ten or more skinny layers with the layer of applesauce between the layers being the same thickness. The top layer did not have any applesauce on it. The finished cake would be kept on the table with a dishcloth covering it for at least two days. The finished product would be very moist because the cake would absorb the applesauce.

While trying to find this cake recipe, as no one had ever written it down, I discovered that this cake had started with the early pioneers of Kentucky and was called a "wedding cake". When there was a wedding people came for miles around to attend the service and celebration. Each family that attended the wedding brought along one layer of cake. The family of the bride probably made the filling out of whatever ingredients that were easily obtained such as apples. The cake would be put together at the wedding and shared by all.

Leona also made regular cakes with powdered sugar icing for birthdays. I was an avid audience. The proudest day was for me was when she let me make a birthday cake, following her direction, for my older brother Roger.

My brothers and I, along with dad's sister Pauline's children, would spend time with Mamaw and Papaw Cloud at their house in the summer when there was no school. We were allowed to sleep over some times. There were a lot of times that dad would forbid us from going to their house. If we disobeyed he would use his plow lines to give the boys a whipping. I can only think that maybe he had an argument with Papaw Cloud or Papaw made a comment to him about us eating him out of house and home.

He and his sister Pauline fought a lot, especially when Pauline was visiting Mamaw and Papaw after she moved back to Dizney. Pauline would bring her children to Mamaw and Papaw Cloud's house. No one ever knew the reasoning behind daddy's actions. Maybe he thought that adding his kids to the number already at their house was just too much aggregation for Mamaw and Papaw. Truth probably was it would have been too much for him so he thought everyone thought like he did.

Papaw went to bed very early so we would have to be very quiet if we wanted to stay up and watch television when we slept over at their house. He would yell from the bedroom if we got too loud for us to turn the television off and go to bed.

I never saw Mamaw or Papaw Cloud hug or kiss. Never remember them calling each other honey or sweetheart. I can see now why daddy never learned to show affection either. Mamaw would keep us laughing by making comments back to Papaw under her breath.

Every summer in the 1950s lots of relatives would come to visit. Berry, dad's brother, his wife Mildred and their children would come home for the 4th of July holiday. Terry and Dennis were the same ages as me and my brother Roger. It was fun playing with some new faces. I didn't like their accent though. They were from Chicago, Illinois. I thought they were talking in that accent to make us look dumb.

Mamaw and Papaw would buy soda pop and ice cream from the store. There would be wonderful big meals made with vegetable from the garden and fruit that had been canned by Mamaw. There would be hams, baked chickens with cornbread.

One summer Papaw's sister came in for the summer and spent a week or so with them. Ida was her name, I believe. She had made a lot of crochet doilies and asked me and Sheila to walk around the entire town and sell them for her. Sheila and I spent the whole day going from house to house and sold some of her doilies.

Papaw Cloud bought a television in the mid 50s. During the day when mom was working at Mamaw Cloud's house, they would take a break every now and then to watch and listen to soap operas while they worked in the kitchen, Some of the soap operas were a continuation of the radio soap operas that they had listened to on the radio in the 30s and 40s. The television just put faces to the voices. Sheila and I learned a lot about life from watching those soap operas.

Mamaw's brother Clark died and left her his money. Clark was divorced from his first wife for many years. Leona learned what it was like to be financially independent for the first time. She bought herself pretty clothes, shoes and jewelry. She started taking trips out of the hills to visit family and friends.

In 1960 we moved to Louisville. Mamaw Cloud missed us something terrible. My brothers and I had a terrible time adjusting to life in the city and really didn't think of anyone except ourselves and didn't realize how much it hurt for Mamaw and Papaw to see us move away.

Roger did not like the Louisville schools. In junior high school he got bad grades and then when he went to high school he began to skip school. When mom got a notice from the school she was really upset. She promised Roger he could quit school if he just finished out the year of school. Our cousin Lanny, Sheila's brother, talked Roger into going back to Dizney, living with

Mamaw and Papow Cloud and going back to school. Roger went back to Dizney in 1964 and graduated at the top of his class in 1967. He graduated one year after me, but he was supposed to graduate one year before me.

Donnie didn't do very well in school either. After Roger graduated and left for the Navy, Donnie decided he wanted to go back to Dizney and stay with Mamaw and Papaw Cloud and finish high school. Donnie went back in 1968 and graduated in 1970.

In 1962 Grandma Presley passed away. Only daddy was able to come home for the funeral. My mom was very upset that she couldn't go to the funeral because she loved her as if she was her own grandmother.

Papaw died in 1972. Mamaw lived in her house with her son Berry. Berry had a drinking problem and sometimes Mamaw had to go visit her daughter Lola or us in Louisville just to get some peace and quiet. Leona had a heart attack in 1988 and died on October 4, 1988. Berry stayed in her house by himself. He died of cancer on May 17, 1989.

Sheila's sister, Andrea and her husband moved into Mamaw and Papow Cloud's house and lived there until their sons were in high school. They bought a trailer and moved out of the holler near her mom, Pauline.

LEONA PRESLEY CLOUD

LEONA PRESLEY CLOUD & TILMAN THOMAS CLOUD

31

Tilman Thomas Cloud, Jr.

Junior Cloud was born August 1, 1925. Junior was the first born of Tilman and Leona Cloud. They lived in Kenvir, Kentucky until Junior was three years old. They moved into a log cabin in the head of Stretchneck Holler in 1928. A couple of years later Tilman bought the house just below where they were living. There were other Cloud relatives who lived in Stretchneck Holler at that time

The other siblings of Junior were Lola, Berry, Pauline and Lora.

Junior was spoiled rotten by his mother. If there were only three eggs for breakfast, Tilman, Leona and Junior would get the eggs.

I am sure that Tilman worked Junior very hard as a child. At eight years old Junior built the fire place in their home while Tilman supervised.

Junior Cloud was a bully and instigator. He knew how to connive to get someone else to do his dirty work. He was the brains behind the worker bees.

At 16 he was bully and teasing a younger boy. The boy had had enough and went home and got his father's pistol. He stood on the mountain and shot daddy as he was walking up the holler. The only means of transportation to a doctor or hospital was horse and wagon. Junior went to church with his parents until he moved away from his home when he was 18. He didn't move far just out of Stretchneck holler to rent a house on the main highway in Dizney. His sister Lola moved with him.

His life was working in the mines and partying on the weekend. He was a very handsome man and the young and older women were crazy about him.

He didn't like having to take care of himself. Cooking, washing and ironing his clothes didn't appeal to him after being waited on by his mom for the time he lived at home. He decided he needed a wife to take care of him.

He noticed a beautiful young girl named Irene Hale. She was in a bad situation at home. There was not enough to eat and she felt she was a burden on her family and was taking food from her younger brothers and sisters.

Junior Cloud proposed by asking her if she would like to keep house and cook for him. Irene being very naive said yes. She considered herself to have been as dumb as a stump.

It took Junior several years to settle down to married life. He felt he could still do whatever he wanted. So he continued to fool around with the ladies. He had to leave town and go to Michigan because a coal company boss found out Junior was fooling around with his wife.

He came back and took mom to Michigan. Junior would go off partying every night after work and leave mom and baby roger alone in the apartment. Irene did not like living in Michigan and demanded to be taken home.

The only place they had to go when they came back to Dizney was move in with Leona and Tilman. This did not work out as Irene was pregnant again and not happy living with her in-laws. Tilman gave Junior the land below his house and loaned him enough money to build a house for his family.

Junior built the house himself. The house had no running water. Junior tapped into Tilman's electrical line. So there was electricity, dry sink and outside toilet. There was no such thing as insulation for the homes. In the winter unless you were in the kitchen when mom was cooking or in the living room next to the stove, you froze. The winds howled and came in through cracks in the walls, floors, windows and doors.

Daddy and his friend had plans to go off drinking. His friend came to the house and made some excuse that he needed Junior to help him do something. Mom was pregnant and from somewhere got the courage to fight back. She got Junior's pistol. Pointing it at Junior's friend she told him to leave her house. She followed him and Junior out on the porch and when his friend didn't leave fast enough she raised the gun and fired in his direction and continued to fire at him as he ran out of the holler. I don't think he came back to the house for a long time.

Daddy worked in the mines when there was work. He did many things to keep us from starving. Some things would be paid cash money, and some things were bartered.

Dad and Uncle Elmer Presley (his mother's brother, who lived below our house) opened a mine and dug out coal and shared it. Later dad opened the other side of the mine below our house to get coal. This was done when he was laid off from the coal mines or the price of coal was too expensive.

Junior's Grandfather Ben F. Cloud was a blacksmith and had his own shop above Tilman Cloud's house. He made horse shoes and tools. Junior did not learn that trade but he could shoe any mule or horse ever brought to him no matter how mean they were.

There was a particular horse that did not like Junior and was trying to bite him or kick him. Daddy hit her between the eyes with his fist and he didn't have any more trouble. Junior made Roger and Tony stay with him while he was shoeing the horses. Tony was scared of Daddy and the horses and mules. Junior was a hard task master and had no sympathy or patience for timid little Tony. Roger learned to hide his fear in a tough exterior.

Junior would slaughter our hogs, his father's hogs and anyone else who needed to hire him to do this. I hated it when November came and he would get ready to slaughter a hog. A big fire was built below our house between the dirt road and the creek. There was a fairly large area beside the road where cars could turn around to go back out of the holler.

Large rocks would be carried or rolled into a circle. Junior would start a fire and keep adding dried tree branches until he had a roaring fire going. Roger carried water from the creek and fill up the washtub with water. The fire served two purposes, one to keep us warm and hot water helped to loosen the hairs on the pig's skin so they could be scraped off with a butcher knife. Daddy had several knives. One had a yellow handle and he carried it all his life.

The weather had to be cold so that the meat would not spoil before it could be cured or eaten. We tried not to get too friendly with the pigs because it was hard hearing or seeing daddy shoot them in the head. He had a triangle made out of three heavy logs tied together at the top. The hog would be shot in the head. A rope was in position at the top of the triangle. The rope hanging down in the middle was tied to the hogs hind legs and the hog was raised off the ground by pulling on the other end of the rope which was hanging on the outside of the triangle.

A second large washtub would be placed underneath the head of the pig. Daddy would cut the pig's throat and let the blood run out of the body into the washtub. He would then cut off the pigs head and let it fall into the tub. Junior would cut the pig from the testicles to the throat. He would pull open the chest of the pig and cut out all the intestines, heart, liver and lungs.

No part of the hog was wasted. The intestines were saved for some of Junior's black friends that he worked with so they could make chitlens. The liver, heart, and hogs tail were saved. The hog would be cut into the separate portion just like a butcher would prepare, such as tenderloin, ribs, bacon, roasts. The skin would be removed and mom would cut the skin into strips, salt them and bake them in the over. They were called pork rinds.

Daddy's father, Tilman Cloud Sr. had a smoke house in his yard. Some of the meat would be salted, smoked and hung up to the rafters. This would cure the outside of the meat and preserve it. The meat would be left hanging in the smoke house until it was needed for one of our family's meals.

After I heard the gun shot that killed the pig, I would venture out of the house and down the road to watch with everyone else. That was not a good experience the first few times, but soon we children got used to it.

When I began to get cold I would walk back up the road and go into the house to sit in the warm kitchen with mom. Mom would get the fresh meat that needed to be cooked right away. One of the things me and my brothers loved was when mom made pork rinds. My mom would cook pork tender-loin and bacon for breakfast. Mom made the lightest and most delicious bis-cuits you ever tasted.

Daddy learned to be a mason at 8 years old. Papaw supervised his build-ing of the chimney to the fireplace at their home. Daddy was very good at building rock walls. Our house was built on the side of the mountain next to the road in Stretchneck Holler. The road was very steep at this point and our yard next to the road had a rock wall that at the highest point was over thirty feet. The purpose was to make the lower half of our house level. The other purpose of the rock wall was to hold back the dirt and rocks of the mountain and keep our house safe.

As the elevation of the road continued up the road to our barn and the steps to our yard the rock wall got shorter and shorter until our front yard and side of the mountain met the road. There were two wooden steps up from the road to our yard.

The road followed the left side of the creek all the way to Papaw Cloud's house. Daddy built a rock wall behind our barn which set between the road and the creek. This kept the spring floods from washing away the dirt behind the barn and the barn itself.

Daddy never owned a moonshine steel that I know of (he definitely knew where to find one when he had the money), but I do remember him making his own beer or homebrew as it was referred to. I remember sitting on the floor of the unfinished large room at the back of our house. I followed daddy around whenever he was home. One time he and I were down at the barn. He was working on something and drinking something from this gallon glass jar. He gave me a sip but I didn't like it.

He decided that I would take a walk with him down the road to Uncle Elmer's house. This was Mamaw Cloud's brother who lived a few hundred yards below our house. Daddy was not so steady on his feet. I don't know how long he had been drinking. He tripped half way to Uncle Elmer's house, knocked me down and fell on top of me. He got up and kept on walking, and did not even know I was lying there in the middle of the road all scrapped up and crying.

After crying for a while, mom came to see what had happened. I learned to stop following Daddy around when he had been drinking.

My father used to make a competition with me and my brothers. I think he did this as a way to strengthen my arms more than anything. I was also a very competitive little kid. He would hold up the broom stick and I would do chin-ups. I remember one time in particular that I did do more chin-ups than my brother Roger.

Later on in life Daddy became a bee keeper like his father. He enjoyed nature very much. His love of the earth and all its creatures was in his genes from his mother's father Andrew Jackson Presley whose grandmother was a full blooded Cherokee Indian. He loved to sit next to the bee hives and watch them fly out in their search for nectar and fly back. He could tell by the direction they took what kind of trees or bushes they were collecting nectar from. He also could tell by the color of the honey what type of tree or plant it was made from.

Dad loved to take his gun and his dogs and go to the mountains. He dug wild onions or garlic called "Ramps" by the locals. It had a very pungent odor but tasted really good. Unfortunately, it left a very bad smell on your breath also. In the spring all the students at the local grammar school were warned that if they came to school smelling like ramps they would be sent home.

Another wild plant that was picked in the spring by the sacks full was poke salad. This was a wild plant that could be cooked and eaten when it was just starting to grow and was still small. This plant could grow to four foot and get purple berries on it. At any stage other than in its early growth this plant was poison if you ate it.

Early settlers learned from the Indians what plants, berries and roots were eatable, medicinal for human beings or animals. Without the help of the Indians they would have surely starved to death and died from lots of causes.

Ginsing the root herb that was so valued in oriental countries grew wild in the mountains of Kentucky. If we needed money and didn't have enough to buy something, daddy would take trips to the mountains digging up "Sang" as he called it.

The Ginsing would be dried in the summer sun during the day and brought in the house at night so it wouldn't be stolen. Daddy was a mean son-of-a-gun when he wanted to be, so I doubt that anyone ever thought of stealing anything from him. In the fall when the Ginsing was dried out it would be taken to whoever bought it and daddy would come home with money. The price would vary depending on the demand.

We raised a big corn crop every summer. Corn was the main staple in our diets. We would eat some fresh picked. The rest was cut off the cob and cooked into cream of corn. Fresh canned cream of corn tastes nothing like what you get in a can today. It tastes exactly like eating fresh off the cob. Some corn would be dried and fed to the pigs. Some corn would be ground into meal which was another staple of our diet "Cornbread". Daddy bought an old car that still ran and hooked the engine up to a grinding mill and people would pay him to grind corn meal for them.

When we lived in Stretchneck and were big enough to hold a pistol, Daddy would put up bottles and teach us to shoot and break the bottles. He taught mom how to shoot when they first got married. Roger had his own shotgun when he was around ten years old and would go hunting by himself.

Daddy was a very good shot and entered many contests. One that I remember most would be the annual Turkey shoot. He won many Thanksgiving turkeys for us. Daddy was also an outstanding gambler. He would come home three sheets to the wind and mom would help him count his money. She counted out some money for mom, (without him seeing her slip it under the table), and some for him.

Junior and some of his friends would go to the mountains and sometimes stay gone for a few days. They would spend time hunting Ginsing, picking ramps, hunting animals like rabbits and squirrels for food.

Junior always carried a pistol and a big yellow handled knife in his pocket. He would tease every kid in Dizney by threatening to cut off their ears with his big knife. Little kids were not the only ones afraid of him. There were a lot of adults who did not mess with Junior or any of his family.

In the summer there would be lots of salesmen, hobos looking for work, people selling peaches and such from their trucks. The hobos and salesmen daddy would scare to death and they would leave Stretchneck in a hurry. Junior liked to pull his gun or his big knife from his overall pocket and tell them they had no business in his holler. These traveling salesmen sold things like socks, bibles, household goods, household linens and curtains, sewing notions. They were not welcomed into many houses in Dizney.

When Junior and Irene's first child died they were both brokenhearted. When I was born it was like Daddy had gotten another chance to have a little girl. Irene had a cat and one time Junior found the cat sitting on my chest when I was still a baby. Not a smart cat. Daddy took it outside and shot it.

Junior seemed to always be in danger of loosing me. At 11 months old I contracted polio and became very sick. Took them awhile to find a doctor who could tell them what was wrong with me. I would have to endure years of surgery. At six years old I fell off the front porch steps and landed on a piece of broken glass from a broken canning jar. The glass cut one of the main arteries in front of my ear and I almost bled to death. I lost over half the blood in my body before daddy could get the bleeding stopped.

My father and I were very close when I was little. I remember how handsome he was. He taught me to count in my mind instead of on a piece of paper. I followed him around a lot.

There were lots more minor injuries to me. Two broken arms, lots of cuts and scrapes, wrecked on a bike and hurt myself. My brother Tony rolled a rock down the side of a hill. It hit a rock and bounced into the air. The direction changed in mid air and the rock hit me in the knee of my good leg and cut it open. Tony cried and begged me not to tell daddy what happened. Tony knew that he would get a whipping. I am sure that daddy gave the boys orders to take care of me when I was with them whether near the house or following them to the mountains.

When we moved to Louisville and I became a teenager. Daddy and I grew apart. When I was in high school, mom left daddy and we moved to another apartment to live. I cried and cried. I missed him so bad. I thought it was the end of the world and I would never see him again. Not so. Daddy would find out where we were living and talk mom into coming back and then another fight and we would be moving again. Mom and Dad got divorced shortly before I got married and moved to New Jersey. Every time I came home to Louisville to visit mom, I would find out where Daddy was living and go see him.

Five years later Junior and Irene were remarried, and had moved back to Stretch Neck Holler into a trailer where our old house used to be.

Daddy was so mean that I am really surprised that he lived to be 78 years old.

TILMAN THOMAS CLOUD, JR.

TILMAN THOMAS (JUNIOR) CLOUD, JR.
AND ROGER LAVOY CLOUD

32

Elmer Farley and Maudie Durham Presley

Uncle Elmer used to be on his porch whenever I would be walking up the holler on my way home from school or visiting my Aunt Pauline's house. I would stop and take a rest on his porch and we would talk. He was so easy to talk to and I liked him a lot. He was a very easy going person. I only heard him yell a couple of times and that was once at Larry and one time at Maxine.

Aunt Maudie was a very reserved person. If I was with my mom and we stopped to rest on their porch, Aunt Maudie would come out onto the porch and talk to mom.

When I was very young I can remember Uncle Elmer and my dad working in Grandma Presley's corn field. They would help with hoeing the corn and then again would be there to help harvest the corn at the end of the summer.

Uncle Elmer was a wonderful husband. He would wash clothes for Maudie, help her with cleaning the house. I am talking about a time when there were certain jobs for men and certain jobs for women and the lines were never crossed. My mom would have to carry her own water from the creek to the washhouse. Carry all the clothes to the wash house. She hung everything on the line by herself with no help from my dad.

I don't remember Uncle Elmer ever going off to work. He must have been retired because he was always home. He and Maudie were not the type to run the road and gossip. They mostly stayed at home and minded their own business.

Daddy and Elmer would help each other out whenever one or the other needed help. One time daddy and Uncle Elmer opened an abandoned mine that was between our house and their house. They hauled coal out of that mine because neither one had money to buy coal to cook with or keep our houses heated.

Alene and I were in the same grade in school. Alene was much smarter than me. When she graduated from high school she went to college and became a nurse. We were in the same Sunday school class. My favorite Sunday school teacher was my Mamaw (Leona) Cloud. I just loved hearing her bible stories.

Whenever I could sneak away and not let daddy catch me, I would walk down the holler to play with Alene. She had a play house set up at one end of the wash house. We would play with her dolls and toys. I never had but one doll that I can remember. Alene had a few more toys than I did. Alene had cats. Her cats were so friendly and nice. I just loved to play with the cats at Uncle Elmer's house.

I don't think Elmer or Maudie had a car. I never saw them driving a car. Their youngest son, Larry, got a car when he graduated high school. I believe he took them places they needed to go.

Maxine was a majorette in the high school band. She got to go on trips with the school band and I admired her very much. I thought that she was beautiful and so much fun. She would come up to my house to visit. She would teach me how to twirl the baton around my fingers. Maxine loved Elvis. Once when Elvis was on television Maxine came to our house to see him. She got so excited that she was jumping up and down on the furniture.

Larry was different from the rest of us cousins. He was a little bit slow. I am not sure how much older Larry was than me and my brothers were. I don't remember him going to the Dizney School. He got teased a lot by the bullies in Dizney. As he got older he learned to fight back. We used to tease Larry too but no in a mean way.

Larry had this little red wagon and he used to pull it up the holler to Mamaw Cloud's house (which was the very end of the road in Stretchneck). I remember one time, my brothers and cousins were in the creek near Mamaw Cloud's house picking blackberries. Larry snuck up and threw rocks at us. He would run beside the wagon holding onto the front arm that guided it and then jump in and ride all the way to his house. That was his get away wagon.

Whenever he would come up by our house or Mamaw Cloud's house and get into it with my brothers he would have the last word and jump in his wagon and no one could catch him. Nobody tried either because they knew they would have to deal with Uncle Elmer if he caught them bothering Larry.

When Larry got older, over 18 I guess, he would drive his car to visit relatives. He got involved with the holiness church and would take trips with the church group. On one trip they were down south somewhere to a revival. Their religion believed that they could handle poison snake and not be harmed if their faith in Jesus was strong enough. Uncle Elmer got a call that Larry had been bitten by one of the poisonous snakes. Some church members drove Larry home and just dropped him off and left. Larry was sick for some time and when he got older it was discovered that the snake bite damaged his kidneys. He had to take treatments on a machine to stay alive.

By the time we moved away in 1960, Alene was the only one at home. Most of their children moved away to Ohio except Alene and Larry. Alene lived in or near Harlan. She worked in the area as a nurse. After Uncle Elmer died in the 1980's Aunt Maudie moved to Ohio. Aunt Maudie passed away recently. She was close to 100 years old.

FAYE, LUCY, MAXINE, RAYMOND, MAUDIE, ALENE, ELMER, LARRY &
HELEN
PRESLEY FAMILY

33

James and Rebecca Hale

James Hale was born on November 2, 1902, in Campbell County, Tennessee. He died October 16, 1982 in Harlan County, Kentucky as a result of "Black Lung Disease". Rebecca Hale was born in Campbell County, Tennessee on April 30, 1903. She died in Harlan Kentucky of diabetes and old age in 1992. She was 92 years old.

James and Rebecca Hale moved to Draper (below Evarts) in Harlan County, Kentucky from Campbell County, Tennessee around 1926. Jim's sister and her husband had come to Harlan County a few years earlier. She had written to her brothers about the great opportunities for employment in the coal mines in Harlan County, Kentucky. The Hale family lived in and around Evarts, Kentucky. James Hale worked for the local mines in and around Evarts for several years. In 1946 their daughter Irene and her husband Junior Cloud lived in Dizney, from where he walked to Kenvir to his job in the mines. James and Rebecca decided to move to Kenvir and get a job in that mine. James Hale lived and worked in Kenvir for the rest of his life. I believe he moved there to be close to Irene and make sure that she would be okay since he did not agree to her marrying Junior Cloud.

The house had a front porch that was the same size as the front of the house. As you went through the front door you would be in the living room. A doorway to the immediate left was Mamaw and Papaw's bedroom. In the interior of the house, except for the front door and the back door, there were door openings but no doors. As you walk into Mamaw and Papaw bedroom you noticed that there was a bed, dresser and a chiffrobe.

The living room furniture consisted of a couch, end table and lamp, a chair, a stove for heat and in the 50's there was a television that one of the sons had bought for them. There was an open doorway opposite the front door that led to the second bedroom, which consisted of three twin beds and a chiffrobe.

A door opening in both bedrooms led into the kitchen, which consisted of a sink with cabinets below in front of a window. My aunt Sue and I stood here many times washing dishes and talking about boys and life in general. A big coal and wood burning stove dominated the kitchen. On the stove were round lids covering the area where the fire would be built. There was a special tool that hooked into a hole on the top of the lids to pick up and remove the lids so more coal or wood could be added to the fire. The stove had an area above the cooking surface which was for keeping food warm. In the front of the stove to the left of where the fire burned was the oven. This old stove was made out of cast iron. The heat from the stove kept the kit toasty warm. The remaining items were a kitchen table and chairs and a piece of furniture called a cupboard.

The house was a four room structure with an enclosed back room that was accessed through a door from the kitchen. This used to be the back porch. There was a tiny porch behind the room off the kitchen with steps leading down to the back yard. There was an outside toilet and a wooden structure where the coal was kept. On one side of the yard there was grass and where the grass ended on the left side was a rock wall. The creek was about three feet lower than the yard. On the other side of the yard there were a grassy area and a fence separating this side yard from the house next door. The front yard was not very big, neither were the side yards. The total footage was probably 75 by 100 feet.

The front yard had a couple of trees on the side near the creek, and on the other side were some flowering bushes with lots of perennial flowers and bulbs. A small ditch was dug between the end of the front yard and the railroad tracks. A foot bridge was built over the ditch. After crossing the foot bridge you climbed a small incline to reach the rail road tracks. You could sit on the swing on the front porch and be level with the railroad tracks in front of the house.

James Hale and Rebecca Hale lived in a four room house owned by the coal company that he worked for. I don't remember seeing Papaw Hale dressed to go to work, probably because we only visited on the weekends. Mom's sister Margaret Ann would pick up my mom and me on her way to visit Mamaw and Papaw Hale on Saturdays. Margaret Ann would either take them shopping, to the doctor or clean house for them.

Sue, Tootsie and I would be left to clean up the house while the adults were gone to Harlan. We would wash the breakfast dishes, sweep, mop, and make the beds. There was a tradition in this family including my mother that the beds must be made every morning as soon as you got out of bed. It was considered a sign of laziness of a person who would leave their beds unmade. After all our chores were done we three would turn on the television and wait for American Bandstand to come on. We danced with each other or a broom as we tried to imitate the dancers on Bandstand. We had to keep a watch for the returning family members so that we could shut the television off before they got into the house. Dancing was considered a sin by Papaw Hale. He would have taken his belt to all three of us if he caught us dancing.

Not sure what Mamaw Hale's opinion was, she never expressed too many opinions. She just let Jim be the boss at least that was my memories. He worshiped Mamaw Hale. He babied her and waited on her. Papaw Hale rolled his own cigarettes from a can of Prince Albert. Becky dipped snuff. She carried around her spit can and placed it on the floor beside wherever she sat down.

One of Sue's jobs that she had to do on Saturday afternoon before we could go anywhere was to get the broom, a bucket of soapy water and scrub and rinse the back porch and toilet. Afterwards Sue and I would find a quiet private place and talk. We would go on the front porch and sit in the swing, go for a walk down the railroad tracks to a little candy store. They sold pop, candy and cigarettes. This store also had a pinball machine. There was a restaurant further down the tracks. We would go there to have a pop and listen to music on the jukebox.

Sometimes mom would let me stay over on Saturday night if I had someone to bring me home on Sunday. One of Sue's older brothers had bought a portable radio for Sue and Tootsie in the mid 50s. Sue and I would sit on the screened front porch and listen to stations from Cincinnati and Chicago. We didn't listen to country music. We loved rock and roll.

When I was small and my mom and I would visit her family, if the train came past their house I would cower and try to hide. I was afraid of the noise of the wheels over the rails and of the whistle that the engineer blew.

On Easter we usually went to my mother's parent's house. Papaw Hale would gather up all the kids and lead them over the railroad tracks to the Brittans Creek Baptist Church that he went to. After Sunday school and church everyone would run down the railroad tracks to the playground and look for the eggs that were hidden while we were at church.

After the Easter egg hunt we all would go back to Mamaw and Papaw Hale's house for a big dinner. The children would play outside while the adults ate. This was a southern tradition adults never sat down to eat with the children. The children had to wait until the adults finished eating to eat. After dinner the children would go out to play and the adults would head for the front porch or one of the beds to take a nap.

When I was about four years old, I was pushing someone in the swing on the front porch. There was no railing around the porch. Every time I pushed the swing I would back up closer to the end of the porch. I got to close and stepped right off the porch. I landed on my hands to break my fall. I was in a lot of pain and someone helped me into the house and I lay down on the couch. It seemed like it took forever for mom to return with her parents from Harlan. The next day mom took me to the doctor or hospital. There was a hospital in Black Mountain that was owned by the coal company. I had broken my arm and came home in a cast.

Jim Hale was a very religious man. He was always quoting the bible and singing church songs. I was Papaw Hale's favorite granddaughter, until mom's sister Alice (Tootsie) had her first child, Brenda. By that time I was a teenager and had moved to Louisville. Brenda became his special grand-daughter.

James Hale said grace before every meal whether there was a full table of people or just him. The oldest daughter would have breakfast ready for everyone each morning. James Hale had very strong beliefs which were taught from early childhood. His beliefs were, no dancing, no drinking alcohol, no listening to rock & roll music, go to church whenever there were services, and follow God's 10 commandments.

As his children grew up and had their own children he would let slide the wearing of shorts and short sleeve dresses or shirts (these were sins for women mostly). The church taught that dancing was a sin because John the Baptist was ordered by the King to be beheaded at the request of a dancer. It seemed to me that everything that was fun was considered a sin by the people of the local churches.

Papaw Hale was always happy and singing church songs. He would teach us the bible by referring to passages that pertained to daily life. He was always giving one of us a big hug and telling us how much he loved us. By us I am referring to his children, grandchildren. His answer to all difficulties was that the Lord would take care of everything.

He loved God and going to church. The Church was on the other side of the railroad tracks from his house. The singing of the choir could be heard from the front porch of his house. There were church services on Wednesday night, Saturday night and Sunday morning and Sunday night. Sunday school classes were before the mid-day sermon and evening sermon was held again around 7:00. I went to his church a few times but I liked my church at Dizney better.

On holidays his children usually would come to visit and bring their children. Those were happy times. On Easter he would gather all his grandchildren that were old enough to go with him to church and bring them along. After church services there would be an Easter egg hunt at the playground just down the railroad tracks. After the Easter egg hunt, everyone would go back to the house for a very large meal. I would think that the older married children gave money to cover buying the food for the Sunday meal. Mamaw and Papaw Hale surely could not afford to feed everyone.

I can only remember one fight that I witnessed in Mamaw and Papaw Hale's house. Chick was drinking and got into an argument with Papaw Hale. Hale got really upset and was crying. Chick walked out the door and angrily slammed the front door. I looked out the living room window to see where he was going. I saw him walking down the railroad toward Black Mountain. Into my view came Bug (Chick's younger brother). He stopped in front of the window and raised a pistol pointed at Chick's back. Luckily someone followed Bug outside and grabbed the pistol before he could fire it.

Mom told me stories of what Papaw Hale would do if any of his children got into a fight. You had to either hug and make up or get a spanking from Papaw. He never wanted his children fighting. Maybe he had experiences with siblings being split up because of some argument or disagreement that could never be forgiven. Now Mamaw Hale was another story. If you did something requiring punishment she grabbed a stick of wood used to build a fire and hit you wherever she could hit you. Mamaw Hale lived with an abusive father who almost beat her to death when she was eight years old. She was sent to live with her mother's family to get away from him. She must not have known much love before marrying James Hale. She was abusive to her children the same way she was abused but only if Papaw Hale was not around. My mother seemed to be the one child that she liked the least. She had her favorites of her children and that was only maybe one or two.

Chick bought the house that Papaw and Mamaw Hale lived in and gave them the deed in the mid to late 50's. James Hale got his black lung settlement in the late 1950s. That monthly black lung check and social security check help with their income in their senior years. The coal mines went out of business in 1956. A lot of the people who relied on the coal company for their jobs, moved out of the county and/or the state to find work to support their families.

Papaw Hale bought himself a car when he got his black lung settlement and social security started. He got a license but the girls would not let him drive when they made their trips to Harlan. Mom said he was not a good driver. Papaw Hale eventually succumbed to his lung problem. Mamaw Hale even though she had diabetes most of her adult life lived to be 94.

JAMES WALDEN & REBECCA WOODS HALE
Mid 1950s

34

Irene Hale Cloud

James Hale and his brothers, Bill and Doc, came to Harlan, Kentucky to find work in the late 1920s. After James had worked long enough to save some money he sent for Rebecca to come with the children.

Irene Cloud's first memory as a young child was of being on a train. She was with her mom, Rebecca Hale, her older sister Polly, and her younger brother James Howard. Irene rode in a seat between her brother and sister. Daddy sent for us when he had a place for us to live. We came by train from St. Charles, Virginia to the train station at Evarts, Ky. I remember when we got to the depot Daddy was there to meet us. When the train stopped Irene saw her Daddy waiting for them. She was so pleased to see him. She was about four years old.

Daddy lost his job and things got so bad when I was young, that Daddy took us back to Tennessee to Mom's dad's house. Grandpa Woods wouldn't let us stay with him so we went to Aunt Maude's (Mom sister). Aunt Maudie and Uncle Herman lived not far from Grandpa Woods. They didn't have any children. They agreed to let us stay with them for awhile. We gathered leaves and corn shucks and put them in sacks to sleep on.

The mines got busy and Daddy took us back to Draper where he got a job again. Polly, me and James Howard got the Measles. Polly had a real bad nose bleed and I remember we slept on straw ticks on the floor. The doctor came and put gauze up her nose and the bleeding finally stopped. Then mom had another baby. Willie was next and then Earnest Lee (Chick) we called him.

One time daddy got what was called "bank poisoning". They got that from working in the mines. The nurses at the hospital called him Lazarus because he had sores all over his body. He couldn't work and we eventually got down to hardly any food to eat.

Some of the people living near us must have told the preacher at a church near us that we were starving. Not long after a truck pulled up to our front door and a Holiness Preacher began unloading jars of canned vegetables and different kinds of food for us. We were so happy to get the food. It was as if God himself had reached down and saved us from starvation. There were many times that the Hale family went hungry. The more babies that came meant there was less and less food. We went hungry many times.

When I was in the second grade our teacher's name was Byrd Sargent. On the last day of school he had something to say about each one of us in his class. He said if he ever married and had a little girl he hoped she would be just like me. During school me and Polly got head lice, mom shaved our heads and we wore tam's on our heads until our hair grew back. The boys would grab our tams and run off with them. We would be so mad at them.

There was a store at Draper and two sisters worked in the store. One of the sisters liked me. She said I looked just like her niece. When Christmas came one year she gave me a small doll. I didn't want to take it because no body else at home got anything for Christmas.

In the winter I can remember going to the slate dump and getting pieces of slate, which was not the high quality of coal, and carrying it home in a lard bucket. Our house was so cold you could see the curtains blow. We would fold paper and put them around the window frames.

Polly and I didn't have clothes to wear to school and we could only wear our shoes in the winter. If we wore a hole in the shoes mom would put a piece of card board in the shoe to cover the hole. Three teachers bought cloth and made Polly and I two dresses with bloomers to match and we were able to go to school.

There were lots of coal mines. The one next to Draper was called Kildav. This mine worked when Draper was on strike. Polly and I would walk along the river bank looking for anything we might be able to use. This was where people threw their garbage and things they did not want anymore. I found a pair of patent leather shoes that had no laces. Mom had red ribbon and she put the ribbon in the shoes. I wore them to church and Sunday school.

Mom always dipped snuff. Our neighbor also dipped snuff and Polly would go borrow snuff from her for mom when mom ran out. Polly would sneak some snuff for herself and talked me into trying it. I tried it and then went to play on a tire swing and got terribly sick. Mom laid a quilt on the front porch for me to lie down on and begged me to tell her what had made me so sick. I never did tell on Polly. I never did try any more snuff either. Polly dipped snuff for the rest of her life.

We never had any toys to play with. We would take old rusty cans and flat rocks and build what we called a play house.

When I was 9 years old a family lived next door to us by the same last name as us, but they were not related to us. I started out going to her house a few times a week to do chores for her. In a few months mom had me moved in with the family and I was staying there all the time. I was doing chores for my keep. I never got paid for the work I did.

I had to work very hard for my food and board. The good side to this situation was I never went hungry. Some times I would get hand me down clothes from their daughter Weida. Mr. and Mrs. Hale would take me with them and their children whenever they went somewhere. One summer they went to Harlan to a fair. There was a man with a small plane selling tickets to get a ride in the airplane. I begged Mr. and Mrs. Hale to let me go on a plane ride and they finally gave in. But I was never to breathe a word to mom or dad. I loved to dance. Weida and I would listen to the radio and go to dances when I was a teenager. If I was living at home daddy would never have let me dance as he believed it was a sin.

My family moved from Draper to Evarts shortly after I began living with Mr. and Mrs. Wm. Hale. I did visit my family because it was not very far and I could walk there. When I visited my family it was because I wanted to see my daddy and siblings. Mom never treated me with any love or affection.

I went to visit once and she was ordering clothes for my brothers and sisters from a mail order catalog. I asked if she was ordering me any clothes and she said she was. But when the mail order package was delivered there were no clothes for me. When I started crying and asking where my clothes were, she gave me a whipping with a stick of kindling for crying and making a fuss.

When Irene was 15 her father's brother, who lived in Tennessee, drowned in a lake. This left his wife alone with several small children. Mom took the bus over to their home in Tennessee to help out. She had to wash all of the children's clothes on a scrub board. Papaw Hale found out Irene was being worked too hard and told her to come home.

Mom came back to Draper. She went to Mr. and Mrs. Hale's house to pack her few possessions into a paper bag and started walking to her mom and dad's house. She would never live with the Hale family again. The Hale family moved to Louisville, Kentucky not too long after mom left.

Irene tried to keep going to high school but she soon quit. She was embarrassed by her old clothes and shoes. She hid to eat her lunch because all she had to eat was home made bread with mashed up pinto beans in the middle.

Junior Cloud saw her and started courting. Irene's mother, Rebecca Hale, told Junior all of mom's best qualities to entice Junior to marry her. Irene's father, James Hale, was against her marrying Junior Cloud. His reputation was not the best. Mamow Hale kept at her husband until he signed allowing Irene to marry Junior. Mom really didn't have a choice because she felt that she was taking food from her siblings and taking up space at home without any means to help support her family. Junior had just moved out of his home and needed a wife to take care of him the way his mother always did. James Hale so regretted letting Irene marry Junior Cloud that he refused to sign for any of his children to get married.

Irene was very insecure and naïve. She thought that all men were like her father, who worshiped his wife, was kind to his family and went to church regularly. Boy was she in for a rude awakening. Junior thought getting married shouldn't have to stop his running around with the ladies and drinking. He wanted Irene as a housekeeper.

Junior would come home from working in the coal mines on Friday and expect not only supper to be on the table but his shirts to be starched and iron perfectly. He would get all dressed and out the door he went to meet up with either a lady friend or drinking buddies. Junior was very handsome. His dark good looks came from his Cherokee Indian heritage. The ladies swarmed around him like bees to honey.

Irene hardly ever stood up to Junior because she really had no place to go if she left him. After the babies began to come she knew she could not support them by herself. Their first child was named Sandra. Irene's labor was very long and painful. Sandra did not cry when she was born. Leona, Junior's mother, who helped with the birth would not give up and continued to pat her on the back and clean out her mouth until a very feeble cry was emitted. Sandra was dead the next morning when mom woke up.

The second child Roger was a healthy baby. Then Portia, Tony and Donnie were born. Donnie was the only child who was born in a hospital.

When Portia was almost a year old and learning to walk she became ill. After taking her to one doctor who treated her for an ear infection, I took her to another doctor who diagnosed her having Polio. This was a real blow after having our first healthy daughter.

Junior went to Michigan to find work after Roger was born. He sent for Irene and Roger. Junior had a one room apartment in a tough neighborhood. He would get all dressed up every night when he came home from work and leave mom and Roger alone in the apartment. One night a fight started on the street by their apartment and gun shots rang out. Irene lay in bed holding Roger and praying to be delivered from that sinful place. Irene demanded to be taken home. Junior took them back to Harlan County.

With no where to live we moved in with Leona and Tilman, Junior's parents. Tilman loaned Junior money to build a house a short distance down the road in Stretch Neck Holler from their house.

IRENE HALE
Abt. 1940

IRENE HALE CLOUD
w/PORTIA AND TONY

ROGER CLOUD

DONNIE CLOUD

35

Dizney as remembered by Irene Cloud

Junior went back to work in the mines for a few years but after Donnie was born he went north to find work again. There were times that Junior sent no money home to support me and the kids. Tilman and Leona saw to it that we did not starve.

A letter came from Junior's sister who lived near him in Michigan. The news was that Junior was living with a woman. I wrote to him that if he did not come home I would file for divorce. Junior traveled home on a greyhound bus but was followed by his lady friend who convinced him to return to Michigan. When Junior went back I went to Harlan County Circuit Court and filed for divorce. When Junior got the divorce papers he came home and stayed.

I learned how to build fires in the potbellied stove and to cook on the kitchen coal stove. I learned to milk a cow, to save a portion of the milk to sour and then churn it until butter came to the top of the churn, and the milk turned to buttermilk. I took care of the chickens and learned to kill them with a swift swing of the ax, throw them under a wash tub till they ceased flapping around. I then would pour hot water over their feathers and plucked the feathers until they were naked. I would then cook them for our meal. Another thing that I learned from Leona was how to make quilts. Quilts were made from any old clothes, scrap cloth or cow feed sacks. They were not art work, just what was referred to as crazy quilts. The only purpose was for the quilts to keep you warm in the winter.

When we lived in Stretchneck holler life was not always the best but one good thing was we always had food. (Irene didn't have much food growing up). We had a cow that was our milk and butter. We had chickens. The eggs were for breakfast and baking. A chicken was always killed for Sunday dinner. Sometimes the chicken would be baked, boiled or fried. We had hogs for meat.

Leona and I shared many chores and most of them were done at Leona's house. All the produce from Tilman and Junior's gardens that needed to be canned were combined at Leona's house. A fire would be built outside in the yard and in the kitchen stove in preparation for the canning which lasted for days. We planted potatoes. When the potatoes were big enough we put them in the dairy and they lasted until spring.

In the spring most of the boys and men went into the mountains and dug ramps. They were like a wild onion or garlic. The leaves were flat not round like an onion. They were boiled with a hunk of meat. The smell was not the best but they tasted good. The smell from your breath after eating them would knock a horse over.

Junior's father had bees and we had plenty of honey. We picked blackberries, raspberries and wild strawberries. I canned the black berries. There is nothing better than country food. Junior would buy a bushel of peaches when the truck came in the summer from down south. We had apple orchards that Junior's grandfather (Ben Cloud) and Ben's brothers started in the late 1800's and early 1900's. There were a lot of different kinds of apples to can each spring and fall. The apples were used for cakes, muffins and ate with biscuit, gravy, eggs and ham for breakfast.

Work was scarce and we didn't have very much cash money or very many clothes. The cow feed came in pretty sacks and I made dresses, pillows cases and sheets. I taught Portia how to make doll clothes on my old pedal foot sewing machine. I taught her how to crochet. When she was six years old she would stand at the sewing machine and make her doll clothes. She only had one doll as a child. I made artificial flowers for Decoration Day out of crepe paper and sold them. I sold eggs, butter milk and butter. I would get Blackie Sexton to come in his taxi and take me to all my stops. Junior made extra money by digging Jin Sing in the fall. The roots would be sold as soon as they dried out. This extra money was always used for something we needed cash to pay for, such as to buy parts for the stove or washing machine.

Junior would also make money by shoeing horses and mules, killing hogs, grinding corn into meal for people. When we didn't have money to buy coal, he opened a mines entrance on both sides of the creek below our house. On our side of the creek, he would go in and dig out coal. On the other side of the creek on his Uncle Elmer's land, he and Uncle Elmer would opened up his side of the abandoned mine and share the coal they got out of the mine.

We used to listen to soap operas on the radio at night. My favorite was Portia Faces Life about a female attorney. Portia was named after this soap opera. Before we had electricity we had a battery radio. After electricity, we listened to Amos and Andy, the Lone Ranger and country music from Nashville on an electric radio.

We went to church on Sunday morning for Sunday school and morning services. We went back for Sunday night services. There was also a Wednesday night and Saturday night service that we didn't always attend.

There were men we called "pack peddlers" who would drive to the center of Dizney or take the bus and then walk up every holler peddling their wares. One time we saw the pack peddler coming up the holler. I locked the front door and took the kids to the unfinished room behind the kitchen and didn't answer the door. Junior was not home. We heard our mean dog "Red" who was tied up on a chain in the front yard barking like he was going to eat someone up, and then we saw the pack peddler racing out of the holler like the devil was after him. He probably didn't see the chain, just saw that mean dog come out of his dog house after him.

When it rained Roger, Tony and Portia would play underneath the high end of the house. Our house sat on the side of the mountain and the lower half sat on tree posts. The side against the hill was even with the mountain. There was enough room between the house and the mountain so we could walk around to the back porch.

The kids never had any store bought toys. They made roads underneath the house in the dirt and used cast off pieces of wood for cars. In the winter they didn't play outside in the snow very much because they didn't have really warm coats, shoes and clothes. I had to dry their wet clothes and shoes by the coal and wood stove in the kitchen or I would dry them on a line on the unfinished back room.

Roger and Tony were outside playing or doing chores every day. When the March winds would blow the small rugs on the floor would be blown off the floor from the wind coming in the cracks in the floor

We had a square type stove in the living room and a coal cook stove in the kitchen. The fire in the kitchen would be "banked" so it would have live embers in the morning so it could be started quickly for making breakfast.

In the winter time, I would "bank" the living room stove so it could be started quickly. The living room stove didn't throw off that much heat. To keep real warm you had to sit or stand around it. It would get so cold sometimes in the winter that if a pan of water was left out at night the water would be frozen by the morning.

Roger was the oldest and he had to carry all the coal, wood and water to the house. He helped Junior with the garden. Junior expected Roger to work as hard as he did. He did a man's job at 12 years old. He had to get the cow in the evening for milking. Some times the cow did not come down out of the hill and Roger had to go get her and Tilman & Leona's cow too.

Junior, Roger, and I did all the hoeing and tending to the garden that was on top of the mountain because that was the only flat place except for behind Tilman's house next to the creek which was his garden area. Roger had to help Junior bring all the crops down off the mountain. Roger would stand on top of the produce that was stacked on the wooden bed Junior made that laid on the grown and was attached to the mule. I was scared to death that the mule would get wild and throw Roger over the side of the hill and kill him. They would use "Toe sacks" or usually had a mule to pull the sled. Junior many times came down from the mountain with corn stalks on his back with the corn still on them. We had two crops of corn, one for our animals and one for us to eat.

Junior got a dog called Flip. He was a hunting dog and he loved Roger. That dog followed him everywhere. Roger got a 12 gauge shotgun for his 11th or 12th birthday. Roger would take the gun and Flip to the mountains and hunt by himself. I couldn't help but worry until he came home.

Portia missed a lot of school in the winter when it was snowy and icy. She caught every cold and sore throat that was going around. She also got lice from someone at school.

Elmer Presley had a daughter named Maxine. She would come to our house to see Elvis on T.V. She would really get excited. She would jump up and down on my couch until I yelled at her to stop before she broke it.

Junior went to Michigan to work and we moved out of the holler to his uncle Clyde Presley's house where Portia was closer to the road for school. Grandma Drucilla Presley lived close to us. She would make toast and rice for breakfast for the kids. They loved it.

Clyde Presley had a chicken lot with chicken wire around a large area with wood on top and corner poles to keep it sturdy. Portia was such a tom-boy and usually ended up hurting herself. She was playing with her friend Wanda Graves. Portia climbed up the gate and sat on the top of the cross piece of wood. Wanda went to get down while Portia's foot was still on the gate for support and Portia fell off and broke her arm.

I had to call a taxi to take us to the hospital. Portia had to stay over night and have her arm put in a cast. She also fell off my mother's porch and broke the other arm. No one told her that she couldn't keep up with her brothers, cousins or friends. She didn't let her brace or leg keep her from doing any-thing.

I had to take Portia to Louisville every year for check ups and her opera-tions. The bus ticket was always paid for by the Shriners who supported the hospital in Louisville where she had her operations. We would either take the bus that ran from Dizney or call a cab from Evarts to come and take us to the train depot in Evarts or the bus terminal in Harlan.

One time that I had to take Portia to Louisville we had a big snow storm. I had told Blackie Sexton to come get us. I dressed Portia and put socks over our shoes to keep us from falling. We started out of the holler to meet Blackie. He took us to Evarts but the bus to Harlan didn't come so I got a ride with someone. The car didn't have any heat and we were freezing by the time we got to the Greyhound Bus Terminal in Harlan.

Portia had an operation when she was 8 years old. On the day she was dismissed from the Kosair Hospital in Louisville the hospital was having a big fish fry on the grounds. Portia and I walked around the grounds and got something to eat before we caught the bus back to the house of the family we always stayed with. People were giving Portia money as she walked around on her crutches. I had enough money when we got home to buy her a good warm winter coat.

Mr. and Mrs. Hale, the same family I stayed with when I was young, would always take us to the train or bus station for our trip back home. We took the last train that ran into Harlan. We mostly took the Greyhound bus.

Junior's sister Pauline Grubbs lived in the first house going up stretch neck holler. Her husband Buford loved to tease Donnie whenever he was in for vacation from his job in Michigan. He would pull Donnie's short britches down from behind. One day Buford was carrying two buckets of water when Donnie saw him. Donnie threw a rock and hit Buford on the nose so hard he spilled half of his water. Buford didn't bother Donnie too much after that.

Larry Presley's father was Elmer Presley, Leona Cloud's brother. They lived in the next house down the holler from us. The walk from his house to the end of the road was uphill. Larry would pull his little red wagon up the hill, find him a good rock and crack Roger or Tony in the head with it. He would then jump in his wagon and race down the hill to his house. Those little wagons did not have breaks.

36

The History of M. Jones & Son's General Store and Post Office By: Chris Jones (grandson of Milton Jones)

In the fall of 1935, the Peabody Coal Company employed Uncle Roy Jones as a miner and his brother Milton was working on the tipple crew at mine number 31 at Kenvir. It was during this fall season that Uncle Roy and several other young men from Dizney were squirrel hunting in Rock Hollow on Cranks Creek when Uncle Roy accidentally shot himself in the arm with a shotgun. He was crossing a wire fence. He had placed the gun on a rock, as he crossed; the gun slipped off the rock and hit the hammer, which caused the gun to fire spattering the shot pellets into the underside of Uncle Roy's arm. He was carried out by his friends and family to a parked vehicle. I believe Uncle George Jones was with him. He was taken to the old Harlan Hospital where he was treated. His arm was in serious shape, and after it showed signs of gangrene it was amputated just below the shoulder.

This unfortunate incident, of course, ended Uncle Roy's career in the mines. My grandfather Milt had for sometime wanted to get away from working on the tipple, and since he was still at home and single, he had been saving his money. Somewhere in the months of 1936 Roy and Milt decided to jump in the ring and open their own business. Their father owned two lots of property near the church in "Punkin Center" and he deeded it to them and helped them get a start. Uncle George Jones, an accomplished carpenter, helped build the building that would house Jones Brothers' store. By 1937 they were in business full swing, and were quite successful in their venture. Peabody Coal Company was operating two mines at Kenvir, just below

141

Dizney, and had hundreds on their payroll. The Black Mountain camps and every hollow in Dizney were full of houses and families. The Great Depression was ending and business was good. Jones Brothers was a true old-time general merchandise store and sold about everything one needed. They sold groceries, meats, dry goods, shoes, hardware, feed and seed, furniture, as well as coal oil (kerosene) and gasoline. The Peabody mines issued scrip as a credit system for their employees and this scrip could be traded at the coal company commissary for goods and services. The Jones Brothers store accepted Black Mountain scrip as payment by the miners, but at a 10% discount. In other words, a dollar in scrip bought a dollar of merchandise at the commissary, but only 90 cents at Jones store. The miners a lot of times still saved money through, because the commissary prices were much higher than the independent stores.

In the early months of 1950 the US Post Office at Dizney was moved by the postal officials from the Pace's store, which also had been in operation for many years at Dizney. One particular day, two post office officials came into Jones store and told my grandfather, Milt, they were moving the post office and needed a place to put it. My grandfather, who happened to be in the store, was sworn in a postmaster. The post office was moved to Jones Brother's store and this naturally helped to attract more business as people called for their mail. In about June of 1950 a terrible set back occurred when the Jones Brother's store burnt to the ground. It destroyed everything, and all was a complete loss. The cause of the fire has never been known. It was thought that maybe the wiring got too hot, as it had been a cloudy day, and the droplights had been on all day. Roy and my grandfather had some insurance and they were back in business the next day. The feed room, which was not attached to the main store, survived the fire, and they went to work selling groceries the next day in the feed room. I remember my grandfather said someone woke him up and told him of the fire, he proceeded to go up and wake up Roy and tell him everything we have is burning up. My grandmother said you could hear the canned goods and shells (ammunition) going off and exploding in the fire. The next day, they waited for the cash register to cool off to get the change out of it. The pennies were melted together.

The mail was delivered to my grandparent's living room at the home where I now live. For a while, my parent's living room became the U.S. Post office at Dizney. The Locust Grove Baptist Church at Dizney had hired Pope and Cawood Lumber and Builders at Harlan Kentucky in 1947 to rebuild a new store building. It is the same building standing yet today. In about 1951 Jones Brothers moved into their new building and continued their business. Post office boxes and counters had been purchased from the old Evarts post office building and were now put into use at the Dizney Post Office. In 1958 coal prices dropped and Peabody Coal closed their mines and their doors at Kenvir. 800 men were out of work. The industrial north called with the promise of work and job security. Hundreds of families left the hills of home and sought a better future in the northern states. Business declined, and it was just impossible for two families to make a living out of the store business. In 1960 Jones brothers dissolved and my grandfather bought Uncle Roy's share out. It was, of course, the fact that my grandfather was postmaster I would say that played the biggest choice of him retaining the store and Roy selling out. Uncle Roy went on and got employment with Kentucky Utilities and retired from there. It proved very successful for him. My grandfather operated the store on, and it remained in our family until about 1983. My grandfather had been in the store business for around 46 years when he retired. Different people in the family worked in the store through the years, including Roy and Milt, Ann and Millie, Harold, Brenda and Charlotte, Herman and Sue, Aunt Thelma, Beckham, Virgil, Sandra and me, Chris. There might be some I forgot.

Today I have the original store books through the years and several old items from the store. One of my most cherished items is an old glass Stewart's candy jar that is the only item that came out of the original store that burned in 1950. It just happened to be at my grandfather's house when the fire broke out. My grandmother had a few days before, put the candy into another container and took the glass jar home. She had washed it up and used it to make pickled eggs, as it was just the right size. I still have it today. I also have one of the old benches out of the store. There were three originally and they sat just in front of the post office. I have seen these seats full every morning as the crowds of old timers gathered to wait for the mail to arrive. They are all gone now. I feel as though I have had a great privilege to have been just old enough to clearly remember the store, the post office in the corner, and the old timers coming in every morning. It was a way of life that had remained unchanged, and I was allowed to see it, just before it vanished. I did not know then that it would all so soon be gone. How I wish so many times I could have captured it on film before its demise, but as we often do, we put off things too long.

37

Stretchneck Holler

There are four main hollers that make up Dizney, Kentucky. There is Bills Creek Holler to the left immediately after the curve where Johnny Pace's house stands. Up this holler is the road that leads to the Church of God and cemetery which is behind the church on the mountain.

The Blevins family lived up this holler. Edward and Goldie Blevins parents lived here when I was a small child. Their daughter's name was Brenda. I thought she was the most beautiful girl I had ever seen. Every summer they would come in to visit Ed's parents and mom would take me with her to visit them. Goldie always brought me Brenda's old clothes. It was as if I was transported to a fantasy land with her beautiful clothes. The other families that lived in Bill's Creek Holler are Gilbert, Blevins, Cox, Madden and Graves.

Continuing on down the road past Bill's Creek holler you will pass a few homes and the Jones Family Store on the right just before the Locust Grove Baptist Church on the left. The next holler is just past the church a little piece on up the road on the right. There is a creek that runs out of all four hollers and down the side of the road all the way to the Cumberland River in Harlan, Kentucky. When you get to the bridge on the right, upon crossing over this bridge you will see Stretchneck holler straight ahead.

Going further down Route 38 you will come to Yokum Creek Holler. The families who lived here were Jones, Cornett, and Pace. Continuing past Yokum Creek past the grade school the road ends and Turner's creek holler begins. The families living here were Thomas, Middleton, Soloe, Steele, Singo and Miracle.

Families living along Route 38 and not in any holler were Pace, Jones, Harp, Fultz, Scott, Thomas, Cloud and Thompson. I apologize to anyone that I have forgotten to include.

After crossing over the bridge you will see a wide open piece of land a hundred feet in depth from the creek to the foot of the mountain. Depending upon the mountain range, some spots could only be fifty feet wide. On either side of the bridge at Stretchneck Holler's entrance were the homes of Cloud, Thomas and Presley families. Simon Cloud, Charlie Cloud, and Cecil Cloud lived on the left side of the bridge. On the right side of the bridge lived Jess Cloud, Clay Thomas, Drucilla Presley and Clyde Presley's family. Further down lived Harrison Cloud, my grandfather's brother and his family, just before Yokum Creek Holler. Going west on the other side of the entrance to Stretchneck holler were the families of Cecil Cloud, Simon Cloud and Charley Cloud

Stretchneck holler was close to a mile from the beginning to the end where my Mamaw and Papaw Cloud lived. The dirt road followed the ups and downs of the tiny valley formed by the mountains on each side. The road was level in some spots and steep in other spots as the road followed the terrain. To the right of the dirt road are the creek, and the other mountain range that made up the narrow valley. Between the two mountain ranges is what we referred to as the holler. Sometimes the dirt road and the creek were right next to each other. There were points where there was land between the dirt road and the creek.

In the early 1920s and 1930s this holler was home to Greenberry and Benjamin F. Clouds children and grandchildren, also Elmer Presley and his children lived here.

Continuing up the holler, the first house on the right was a building that was a home to a Casteel family who had a store directly below the house at ground level right at the side of the road. When my mom and brothers and I came out of the holler mom would usually have some pennies that she would give us so that we could buy some loose candy. There were jars on the counter filled with candy. There was a long case filled with candy. The owner also sold cigarettes. My favorite things to buy were Mary Jane candies.

There was a foot path leading around the front of this house and up higher above their house. Up here lived Simon Cloud and his family. Simon was another son of Frank and Mary Jane Cloud who lived just up Stretchneck holler.

The house to the left was set up against the mountain facing towards the highway. The yard was fenced in the 1950s. There were a couple of concrete steps at the edge of the dirt road and a gate to enter. Next to the gate was a building that held the coal for the furnace. There was a concrete walkway that led up to the front porch. The porch was the entire width of the house. This house's first family was Ed and Goldie Blevins. The second family was Will and Mary Ellen Cloud and the third and last family was Buford and Pauline Grubbs (my dad's sister).

There was a basement that I went into with Sheila once and never went into again. I had nightmares of spiders, snakes and mice living down there. There was a wide front yard that got smaller as you walked down the yard towards where it ended. Below the end of the yard was a building. I believe that belonged to this property and at one time was a garage. Behind the side yard and walkway was a long not very wide garden area a little higher up the hill.

The house had six rooms. From the porch you entered the living room. To the left were two bedrooms. One bedroom led into the other one. Straight ahead was a dining room and to the left was the kitchen. Across the kitchen is what used to be the back porch, but later on it was turned into another bedroom.

Continuing on up the holler on the left is Homer and Mary Ellen Cloud's house that sat up against the bottom of the mountain and faced down the holler. The road was very close to the side of the house facing the road and the creek. This area of the dirt road was wide just below Homer's house. On the right of the dirt road were Homer's barn and an area wide enough to pull over should you meet a car coming down the holler. This was a very rare occurrence until the mid 50s.

There was a little foot bridge over the creek to the other side where a house sat up against the rock wall of the mountain facing the road. There was just enough room for the house as I remember. Dan and Lottie Pace lived here. This house couldn't have had more than two rooms it was so tiny.

The road around Homer's house was a steep curve as it hugged next to their house and the mountain. To the right of the road the earth fell straight down into the creek, which was about 15 to 20 feet. The dirt road and creek continued this way for a short distance. The road was level for awhile and was up against the bottom of the mountain on the left. At the right side of the road the land continued to fall straight down to the creek.

Just after the curve in the road straightened out there was a house across a small foot bridge over the creek. Frank and Mary Cloud lived in this house. Their property was about 40 to 50 feet wide. The land followed the creek and the mountain and became smaller in the front and back of the house as the mountain and the creek met again.

Just when the road started to get steep again, there was another dirt road that went back in the opposite direction but climbed the side of the hill until it stopped at Pearl and Tilde Cloud's house on the mountain above Homer and Mary Ellen's house. This was a smaller path that was barely wide enough for a wagon. Mom used to take me with her when she would give Tilde's daughters permanents.

There was a small house on the right side of the dirt road at the point where Pearl's road begins. There were several people who lived in this small house. I remember Lewis and Pauline Cloud Blevins living here. Lewis's father was Jess Cloud. Jess was another son of Frank and Mary Jane Cloud. Also in the mid 60's Dan and Polly moved off the mountain above Mamaw Clouds house to live here because Dan had become ill with cancer.

At this point the road gets pretty steep as we pass the beginning of Uncle Elmer and Aunt Maude's front yard. This part of the mountain at one time came further down past the dirt road and a part of it was cut away to make room for the road and Uncle Elmer's house and front yard. When the road leveled off Uncle Elmer's house was on the right of the dirt road. You could walk right off the road onto Uncle Elmer's front porch. His house set down lower than the road level and there was a fence at the edge of the road going past his house. Behind his house was a small building. Behind that building was his garden and to the left up a little rise that met the road again was his barn.

The creek and the road met at a short distance beyond Uncle Elmer's barn. The road remains flat for a few more yards then goes to the left around a small bend and the creek goes to the right and there is again land between the road and the creek. Just before the road starts to get steep there is a level area large enough to turn a car around and go back down the road. There are only three places in the holler where you could turn your car around and go back out of the holler. Below our house and just below Mamaw and Papaw Cloud's house which was just a few yards above our house and across from Homer Cloud's house.

To the left of the dirt road at the turning place is a small cliff, rock jutting out beyond where the mountain ends. Underneath this cliff is a recessed area as wide as the cliff overhang and a ditch about fifteen feet down to the road. This is the cliff I walked off of when I was little. Only I walked off the short end which was more like three feet, but to me this spot was about 20 feet high.

The road is the steepest as it climbs past my house. My house is a few yards ahead high on the mountain on the left side of the road. The dirt road climbs up past our front yard on the left and our barn on the right. The road starts to level off just past the washhouse on the right next to the creek. Almost immediately the road widens to the right and a large area is here to turn a car around just in front of Mamaw and Papaw Clouds barn. This area was just before Mamaw and Papaw Cloud's house. Beyond this point a car could not go any further. Here is where the road became smaller, more of a wagon trail. The road continued on between Mamaw and Papaw Cloud's house and barn.

To the right and left of the road is Mamaw and Papaw Clouds property. Their house sat up above the road about 8 feet in the beginning. There is a rock wall that went from the beginning of their property past the front of the house, which faces towards the road and ended at the two steps that led up from the side of the road to a concrete walk way. This walk way led to concrete steps leading up to the front door of the house. At the top of the rock wall the front of the house sat back about five feet and was level the entire length of the house.

To the right of the front door is the side yard. The yard is level a short distance to their pump which was in the middle of the side yard. Beyond the pump the yard elevates a little up to their smoke house. The back of the side yard and the house begins mountain range which is very steep. On this side of the house sits Papaw Clouds bee hives and some flowering bushes. Above this area a little higher up the mountain is a paw paw tree.

If you follow the path behind the smokehouse you will go past a long flat piece of land where Papow Cloud planted his garden. The road curves to the right at the end of this garden, and here the creek is the same level as the dirt path. Where the water flows is over a flat rocky portion of the mountain. You can walk through the inch or two of water to get to the opposite mountain range on the right that forms the valley in Stretchneck holler. This is the point where my father would say the holler "heads up" with the mountain. The two sides of the mountain meet here form another mountain range.

After we get across this low stream the mountain on this side begins. Here is a wagon trail that has been cut into the side of the beginning of the mountain. The trail goes back in the opposite direction that we have been traveling and climbs steadily until it gets to the top of this little rise. To the left the land is flat and is probably a couple hundred feet across to the other side where the mountain continues its upward journey. This flat area is twice as long as it is wide. This is where the cows used to graze, and visit their salt lick. Across this field from the wagon trail that led up from above Papaw Cloud's garden was another wagon trail that climbed in the opposite direction until it reached another level area. Up here in this level area sits the cabin where Dan and Polly lived. There is an apple orchard up here. Daddy told me that Grandpa Ben's brother lived in this log cabin originally and had planted the apple trees. Going up the mountain from the apple orchard you will reach the top. If you follow a path to the left at the top of the mountain you will reach my father's garden.

38

Clyde Presley's House

Clyde Presley, Son of Drucilla and Andrew Jackson Presley lived just past grandma up a rise on the same side of the hill that her house was on. His family lived there until the mid 50s. Clyde moved his family to Louisville when the mines closed down. This house stayed empty for a couple of years.

Dad had gone off to Michigan to find work. Mom was finding it hard helping me get out of the holler to the school bus and to church in the rain and snow. So she made an executive decision and moved the boys and me out of the holler to Clyde's house. While we were living there we kept an eye on Grandma Presley.

The only yard to Clyde's house was the dirt area on the side of the house facing Grandma Presley's house. There was a small area of cleared yard below the front porch that faced the creek and county road beyond. It was quite a distance from the house sitting on the hill to the creek. It had to be a few hundred yards. This area was covered in briars, boulders, scrub trees and weeds. There was no venturing into this part of the property.

There were steps leading up to the front porch and a couple of small steps leading into the tiny kitchen at the back side of the house. There was a window looking out from the kitchen onto the rock boulder. The kitchen seemed to have been an after thought and added onto the back of the house after the main house was built.

The back of the house sat about two or three feet from where a huge boulder juttied out from the mountain. The boulder was as wide as the house and not quite as tall as the house. The rock was not like a sheer cliff face but it was round with smooth areas on the side that you could use to climb up to the top. My brothers and I used to love to climb onto the boulder behind the house and chase lizards. They were small dark brown lizards. We would catch them and play with them for awhile and then let them go.

The house had a living room with a door leading onto the porch and a doorway at the opposite end leading into the kitchen. There was only one bedroom. The boys and I slept in the bedroom and mom slept in the living room. She would put us to bed when it got dark and she would turn on the radio. We would fall asleep listening to the Grand Ole Opera, the Lone Ranger and Amos and Andy.

The first winter in this house was terribly cold. The only heat was the kitchen stove. There may have been a small stove in the living room, but I am not sure. There were cracks in the wall boards and the floors. I caught the mumps. The boys got the croup. This was not a memorable time.

The boys did chores for Grandma Presley. She was always finding something for them to do for her, such as bringing in water from the pump, splitting kindling, and carry coal.

Next to the house was a building for tools. After the barn was a fenced area and small building for the chickens. The building was so the chickens could get out of the bad weather and could roost at night. There was a skinny piece of wood on top of the chicken wire fence that surrounded the area. Between the fence and the building was a tall homemade gate with a latch. This is where you would enter the area to feed the chickens and collect the eggs. I don't believe there were any chickens there when we moved here or not.

I was playing with my friend Wanda Graves who was in the same grade as me. She lived in Bills Creek holler. We both had climbed up the gate and scooted out onto the top rail. We sat there for awhile talking. Wanda needed to go home so she climbed over me and put her foot onto the gate to get down. My foot slipped off the gate and I fell down onto the hard ground and broke my arm.

Poor mom had enough problems without me adding to them. She had to call a taxi from Evarts to come get us and take us to the Harlan Hospital. I had to stay overnight and came home in a cast the following day.

My brothers and I would walk home from school for lunch. I don't think mom was getting much money from daddy. We didn't have a lot of food. We usually had pinto beans, fried potatoes and cornbread twice a day. I believe Mamaw and Papaw Cloud were supplying us with food. Mom had probably put out a few tomato plants at this house. But she couldn't take care of us and care for a huge garden like daddy did when he was at home.

One day mom missed Donnie, my little brother, and searched all over for him. She went down the hill to Grandma Presley's house and he wasn't there so she started down past Grandma's cornfield past a few house and he wasn't there either. She decided to walk down the road towards the church house. Half way to the church house she saw Donnie coming towards her walking on the path between the road and the creek. He was carrying a paper sack.

Donnie had gotten hungry and couldn't find anything he wanted to eat, so he decided to walk to the Jones store. When he arrived at the store Milt Jones, the stores owner, asked what he could do for Donnie. To which Donnie replied "mom sent me to get a pound of baloney and a loaf of bread". Milt thought it was kind of odd for the little guy to come by himself. Donnie didn't have any money so Milt said he would put it on mom's store bill.

While we were living in Uncle Clyde Presley's house, mom did not have enough money to buy lunch for us when we went to school. For the first time ever, I would walk home from school with my brothers. We crossed the creek and walked up the hill along the fence that separated this property from whoever owned the land next to Clyde's house. It was spring time and the weather was sunny and warm. We continued coming home from school at lunch time until school ended at the end of May.

Mom would have Pinto Beans, fried potatoes and cornbread hot and ready to eat when we got there. We would have water from the water bucket mom kept filled from Grandma Presley's outside pump. When we were rested and done eating we would walk back to school.

Daddy came home from Michigan while we were living at Clyde's house. He had built some cages. They were made of wood with chicken wire on the front and back ends of the box. He was in the mountains hunting and came upon some rattlesnakes. He decided he was going to catch one and bring it home. What possessed him to do this is beyond me. Daddy cut off a tree limb that had two branches that forked out from the main branch. He tied the snake to the tree limb and brought it home. He put a snake in the wooden cage and left it on the ground near the front porch.

I had always been scared of snakes. I was fascinated by the snakes as long as it was not going to get loose. The cage was in the yard for a couple of months. I liked to watch the snake. I would sit on the ground a safe distance away from the cage. I was particularly interested in how the snake managed to get their old skin off and I got to watch this happen.

Papow was at the house and daddy was no where around when somehow the cage got knocked over and the snake escaped. Mom and all of us kids ran inside the house and closed the door. Papow Cloud found a hoe and managed to kill the snake with out getting bitten himself.

Not too long after that we moved back to Stretchneck holler. I preferred to live in the holler near Mamaw Cloud house anyway.

39

Portia's Many Accidents

When I was small I fell down a lot. My left leg that was affected by the Polio virus was very week. My mother was very protective of me and would run and pick me up every time I fell and started crying. As a natural reaction I began to expect mom to come running and pick me up. I probably liked the attention as any child would.

One day mom stopped running every time I started to cry. I am sure she would look out the window or door to make sure nothing dangerous had happened to me. I did not know that my father's sister Lola had a talk with mom and that was why she no longer ran to pick me up.

Lola had told mom that she was doing more harm than good for me. Lola made mom realize that some day she would not be around to pick me up and then what would I do. I had to learn to rely on myself instead of mom. Especially when I grew up, married and had children. Mom needed to let me start depending on myself so that I would better be able to take care of myself as I grew up and did not need to depend upon mom for help.

Mom did stop running to pick me up, but she was always there for me as long as I lived at home whether in Dizney or Louisville, Kentucky. Mom would always hold my hand or we would cross arms and she would lend her strength to support me when we walked together, as I would get tired quickly and we would have to stop and let me rest my leg.

I did not realize until I got to be an adult this conversation was the best thing that could have happened to me. It made me more independent and I learned to take the hard knocks and get up to try again.

Thus began my independence. I was allowed to play with my brothers and cousins without any oversight. This meant that if I got hurt I couldn't blame anyone but myself. Roger, Tony and I would play follow the leader and I would attempt to do whatever they did. I even climbed up to the rafters on the unfinished room behind the kitchen. We played Cowboys and Indians. Roger would make us a bow out of a tree limb and a piece of string. Our arrows had chicken feathers on the end so that they would fly pretty far. Roger made us darts out of a corn cob, nail and chicken feathers.

One time I followed Roger and Tony behind our house on the side of the mountain. We were playing on the side of the hill when one of the boys disturbed an underground yellow jacket's nest. This part of Kentucky had more bees that lived underground than out in the open on bushes and trees. The bees came out mad as could be. Roger rolled down the hill, under the fence that surrounded our property, and onto the road below the house. Tony ran to the front of the house. I could not run but walked as fast as I could. I was screaming all the way.

Mom came out of the house as I was coming around the side of the house screaming my head off. There were yellow jackets stuck in my curly hair stinging me in the head over and over. I also had stings on my arms and legs. Only a mother could stick her hands into that tangled mess of curls and pull out those yellow jackets. I am sure she was stung several times too.

My parents began to get used to me getting hurt. They could not put me into a bubble. My cousin Sheila and I were running behind the barn, can't remember what we were doing, I tripped over a tree root and cracked my head on a big rock that was on the ground. Sheila led me back around the barn and up to the dirt road and took me to my house. Daddy put a butter-fly band aid on the cut but he didn't bother to clean the wound first. Until this day I can truly say I have rocks in my head even if they were only little pieces. I could feel those tiny bits of rock under the skin above my eye for years.

I tried swinging on a grape vine in the woods up on the hill behind Papaw and Mamaw Cloud's house. Everyone was having a turn grabbing the grape vine on one side of the hill. We would run straight out and pick up our feet when we could not touch the ground and fly into the air and swing across to the other side of the hill. I don't remember how many turns we all took on that grape vine swing. I think I was last one in line. I took as best a run as I could since I really couldn't run anyway, and flew out into the air. Halfway into my flight to the other side of the hill, the grape vine broke and I landed in a bunch of wild briars. I had on either shorts or a dress and got myself scratched up pretty good. I got up brushed myself off and walked home crying.

I broke one arm falling off my Papaw and Mamaw Hale's porch while pushing someone in the swing. I fell off the top of a chicken wire fence and broke the other arm.

Tony or Roger had a little red wagon when we were little. Roger or Tony pulled it high upon the side of the hill above the house. Roger steered and Tony sat in the back and they went flying down the hill. Roger turned to the left as he got to the bottom of the yard just before the rock wall that ran along the side of our yard. Below the rock wall was the dirt road. The rock wall was about twenty feet above the dirt road at the point just below our house and got closer to the road at the end of the yard. Roger turned before the rock wall and the wagon ran long the yard towards the steps that lead to the road and stopped.

Roger and Tony safely ended their ride in the wagon. The wagon was pulled back up the side of the mountain above our house by Tony. This time Tony and I were going to go for a ride. Only when we got to the flat area of the yard, we panicked and did not turn the wheel to the right. We went sailing over the rock wall right into Daddy's arms.

Luckily dad and mom had been sitting across the road in front of the barn watching us play. Dad had a premonition I guess and made it down and across the road in time to catch us. I think daddy threw or gave that little red wagon away, because I don't remember seeing it around after that adventure.

Another time Tony and I were above Mamaw and Papaw's Cloud house and garden. There was an old abandoned mine on the hill to our left and Tony decided he would climb up the hill and see what was up there. He explored a little and decided to roll rocks down the hill. He picked up a piece of slate rock from the mine and rolled it down the hill, but it hit another rock and split in two pieces. One piece went above where I was standing and the other piece took flight into the air and hit me in my good knee making a small cut. Tony had to help me home and begged me all the way not to tell daddy what had happened because he knew he would get a whipping. I, of course, never told daddy and mom cleaned up the cut and kept quiet also because she didn't want to see Tony get a whipping either.

The worse accident I had came when I was five or six years old. It was a typical summer day. Aunt Pauline and her children were visiting at Papaw and Mamaw Cloud's house. My brothers and our cousins were outside in the road between our house and dad's parent's house playing. There was a lot of yelling and laughing going on between them.

I was in the house with mom and dad. I had decided to go outside and play with them. I came out the screen door onto the porch. There was a swing to my right and in front of me were the wide steps, without any railing, that went down to the middle of our yard. The distance on the left side of the steps nearer to the mountain side was only about three or four feet and the other side could have been four or five fee. There were about ten steps from the porch to the bottom of the steps.

When I walked down these steep steps I would usually lead with my good leg and then bring my bad leg down to meet the other leg. I would continue in this fashion until I got to the last step and safely reach ground. I was thinking to myself, my bad leg is getting stronger now, I think I can walk down these steps just like everyone else.

After a couple of steps of switching from left leg to right leg, when I put all my weight on my bad leg my knee gave way and I fell over the side of the steps and landed on a broken canning jar that had fell off the porch wall next to the steps earlier in the day

Earlier in the day mom and Roger were bringing empty canning jars from the dairy to the porch because mom had planned to can some vegetables after daddy went to work in the mines that day. They both walked away and did not notice the box with the jars fall off the porch wall and break when they hit the ground. Unfortunately for me the broken glass never got picked up.

A sharp pointed piece of the Mason jar went into the side of my head just in front of my ear. This was in the area of the main artery to the brain. I could feel the glass slicing into my head. I started crying and screaming, because I am sure it hurt. It took mom a few minutes to come out onto the porch to see what was going on. She looked down and found me lying in the glass. She jumped over the side of the steps, picked me up and carried me up the steps to the porch.

Mom screamed for my dad. He brought a basin of cold water to wash the blood away so he could see the cut. As I looked at the basin and the water was turning red with blood. I could not comprehend what had happened and how much danger I was in if the bleeding could not be stopped. My dad stuck his thumb into the wound and pushed hard until the blood stopped flowing. There was blood on the ground, steps and porch. Once the blood stopped flowing, dad holding my shoulders and head with his thumb still stuck in the side of my head and mom holding onto my legs hurriedly began carrying me out of the holler looking for some help.

My Mamaw Cloud heard all the screaming and carrying on but didn't decide to come down to our house until after mom and dad had made it half way out of the holler. She came into the yard saw all the blood and fainted dead away onto the ground.

Stretchneck Holler was given that name for a reason. The first person to come out of their house to see what was going on was Uncle Elmer, Mamaw Cloud's brother. He and I had a special friendship and were very good friends. He probably didn't think he would be seeing me again.

It was almost a mile from our house to the end of the holler by the big bridge. There were at least five or six more houses to pass. I don't remember anything after Uncle Elmer coming out to see what had happened to me. When we got out of the holler there were quite a few houses up and down the creek on either side of the big bridge. There were a few cars parked near the bridge. Mom opened the back door to one of the cars and sat me down on the seat. I got sick to my stomach and stuck my head out the door and threw up on the ground. Daddy must have gone to one of the houses to find the driver of that car to take us to the hospital. I don't remember the ride to the hospital.

The next thing I knew I was sitting on a bench in a hallway in the hospital in Black Mountain. Mom was sitting next to me and daddy was talking to the nurse. I had dried blood all over me and my clothes. My hair and dress was stiff with blood. I don't remember us seeing a doctor. We were suddenly in a room with a bright light over the table I was laying on. I must have been put to sleep or my head numbed. I started seeing Tony and Roger in the room with me but they were hanging upside down on some kind of bars. The doctor stitched me up and gave me a few pints of blood. The doctor told mom and dad that I had lost over half the blood in my body and would have died in another few minutes if daddy had not stopped the bleeding.

Funny thing about dad and the first aid he applied to save my life; any man applying for a job in the coal mines had to pass a first aid course before they got hired. Daddy took that first aid course three times before he finally passed the test. Good thing for me he had to repeat the course three times. At least he remembered what he had to do to stop the bleeding.

When I was brought home, mom made a bed on the couch for me and I didn't move for about a week. When dad was at work mom could keep and eye on me from the kitchen since the entrance was an open space with no door just two half walls on either side of the opening into the kitchen. When dad came home from working in the mines he slept on the floor next to me until I was recovered.

I guess it took me awhile to get back into the thick of things with my brothers and cousins. I was not limited to staying close to home so I wouldn't get hurt again. I was always given unlimited freedom, but that did not include going out of the holler alone. Dad was always trying to protect me without hindering my freedom to play and do whatever my brothers did. That included follow the leader and jumping off the roof of the house onto the side of the mountain that was next to the house.

Daddy tore down the front steps. He closed up the opening on the porch where the steps were. He had always had the end of the porch next to the mountain opened so we could walk right off into the yard. That became the only way to get off the porch.

40

Summertime

Memorial Day weekend or Decoration Day, as it used to be called; was the end of the school year, and the beginning of summer. It was great to not have to get up early and go to school. Breakfast came later in the morning unless mom had work to do and needed to get breakfast over with early. For me the day was usually enjoyed just lazing around and day dreaming. Roger and Tony had jobs to do. I usually followed mom around and watched her cook, iron, sew, crochet, clean and I would help when she would let me.

I also loved to be outside in the sunshine. I remember smells and sounds like they are pictures in my mind. Just laying down on the ground and closing your eyes you could feel the warm sun on your body and hear the bees buzzing around, their wings flapping double time. I was afraid of bees. Papaw Cloud had beehives for honey. Every time he raided their hives, they were mad for a few days and would fly around looking for a human to sting even yards away at my house (which was down the road within yelling distance).

There were lots of different kinds of bees. There were wasps that built dirt homes under the eves of our house. There were yellow jackets that built their homes in the ground, and hornets who built their paper nests in bushes and trees. The wasps built their paper homes usually around wood structures such as barns, outside on houses, toilets, chicken coops and hog pens. It was always a good idea to look inside of the toilet before you went in and closed the door.

There were big large bumble bees that were yellow and black that never bothered anyone. My dad always told us to not bother the bees and they wouldn't bother us. Dad respected all of God's creatures as they had a job to do in the scheme of things. The bees were necessary to pollinate the garden, the trees, the flowers, all growing fruit and all things that had flowers.

While lying on the ground you also could hear the flies droning. Flies made up the largest population of insects and bees. They were very noisy. I guess there were more flies because they lay their eggs in all the animal dung and toilets.

We loved to catch June bugs and tie a string to one of their legs. This way we could control their flight near us. Crawling ants could be really mean. There were the small black ones, the red ones and the large black/brown ones. Some of the ants you did not want to mess with. If their homes in the ground got disturbed they would come out mad as a honey bee when his honey was stolen. The red and big black ones could bite and really hurt. If you got 20 or 30 crawling up your legs you were in deep trouble. Bugs and spiders could be heard rustling through the grass if you were lying down on the ground.

My favorite was listening to the birds singing and trying to recognize the bird. There were Robins, Blue Birds, Pheasants, Mawking Birds, Woodpeckers, Hawks and Buzzards, too many to list. I used to love to lie down on the ground and watch the chicken hawks and buzzards fly above me in the sky. I still like to watch the birds in flight.

The smell of warm sunshine made the heart soar. The smell of the earth when it was damp from a rain was a different smell from earth hot from the summer sun. Grass and weeds underneath and surrounding me as I sat or lay on the ground were a comforting smell. Everything had a special smell from the wild fruit, flowers, and the trees in bloom to the smell of the cow, pigs and chickens that we raised.

We always had dogs. They were used by daddy for hunting small game in the mountains. They were valuable for finding rabbits, and squirrels for food and the dogs could smell a snake before any human could. They were also for protection in the woods and around our home. They would let us know when someone was walking up the dirt road toward our house or anyone in the woods near our house. Dogs were not to be petted as that would make them unfit for their jobs. When dad was not around we did treat the dogs like family. The dogs got to eat the scraps from the meals we ate and if they were lucky daddy could afford to buy them a bag of dog food every now and then.

The cow was important as it gave us our milk and butter. They also would step on any snakes near them and kill them before they got too close to our property. Mostly their smell was an earthy smell from lying on the ground. They were very sloppy eaters with their mouths dripping juices from whatever they eat whether it was an apple or weeds. The cow was special because they got store bought food and sometimes dried corn on the cob. The feed came in large cotton bags that had pretty patterns on them. The bags were used to make clothes, curtains and even quilts. I loved the smell of their feed that the cows ate. It smelled good enough to eat and I did. I was far too curious for my own good sometimes.

The chickens had their own special place. Daddy always had chicken coops for them. Their coops had roofs and three sides. The front of the coop was open so that we could walk around them and collect the eggs. Sometimes there were small individual houses just for the chickens that hatched their eggs. Their opening was only big enough for them to get through the hole.

There would be tree branches without their leaves for roosting and some spots that had long boards with straw or grass on the bottom where the chickens could sit and lay their eggs. There was always a fence encircling the chicken coop to keep wild animals from killing and carrying off the chickens. If daddy heard them making a ruckus when he was around he would run for his gun and make a bee line to check out what was upsetting his chickens. In the warm weather there would be tiny baby chickens marching around following their mother. They were so cute. My brothers and I would hold them when daddy was not around.

The chickens picked every blade of grass in their area until there was nothing but dirt. The chicken feed would be thrown around on the ground inside their enclosure for them to eat. The smell from their craps was terrible and when collecting eggs you had to watch where you were stepping to avoid stepping on their crap.

We had a barn that daddy built across the dirt road from our house. The barn was between the road and the creek. The barn had its own smells. There was a door in the middle of the rectangle shaped barn. Upon entering you walked onto a dirt floor. There were enclosed areas on both sides, with a wooden half wall about three feet high and a gate to keep the animals enclosed. Usually in the wintertime the cow and mule stayed in these pens to keep warm and dry. Straight ahead was a step up to the wooden floor of the barn. There was an opening in the wall on the right side where you could look into one of the pens. Here was where daddy kept his tools, plow, mule halters and reins. This is where he kept everything that didn't belong in the house, his stuff. He had his tools needed to shoe horses, butcher his pigs, plow and hoe his garden, and grind his corn into meal for cornbread

There would be corn piled into a corner waiting for it to dry and be ground into corn meal for cornbread or left whole to feed the pigs or cows. His tools smelled of rust, oil and dirt. Daddy always kept his tools and guns in good working order. Daddy made extra money shoeing other people's horses or mules and he ground corn into meal for people. The smells of the barn were earth, mold, metal, corn, cows feed, old wood planks, oil needed to keep the tools sharp. The other smell was not that great and that was the smell of mice, their droppings and their nests. Mice were always around.

The creek was one of the centers of our life. Mom carried water from the creek to her wash house to wash clothes. The wash house was next to the barn and close to the creek. The animals drank water from the creek and so did my brothers and I if we were above Mamaw and Papaw Cloud's toilet as they were the last house in the holler or in the mountains. When it was hot my brothers and I would go to the creek to sit in the water to cool off. There was no place in Stretchneck holler that was deep enough to swim. Each summer the older boys and girls would dam up the creek in areas where it was wide and deep enough to swim. This would usually be in the larger main branch of the creek that flowed down to Harlan, Kentucky and into the Cumberland River.

During the fall, winter and spring we would get rain storms that would cause the creek to flow fast and furious. The depth of the creek would also rise and sometimes cause floods. The sound of the rushing water could be so loud it dominated all the other sounds outside of the house. In the summer the creek would get really low and the only sound would be a gurgle or a splash from the minnows playing with each other or trying to escape the mouth of a water snake. Other prominent sounds were the constant noise the water made as it washed over the rocks on its way to the mouth of the holler and into the tributaries that ran into Yokum Creek from every other holler in Dizney. The water was cold all the time.

The creek had a life of its own. The creek bed was rock with silt at the bottom of the water with slippery moss growing on the wet rocks. There were tadpoles that swam around and eventually became frogs and moved onto land. There were small crayfish which we called "crawdads". Never go into the water barefoot if you see "crawdads". When they pinch they don't want to let go. There were tiny minnows that swam in the water. If anything disturbed the water the minnows would dart into the crevices of loose rocks to hide. The minnows never grew large enough to catch with a fishing pole. We hardly ever caught them in our hands because they were too fast. If someone was fast enough to catch the fish it was usually put back into the creek water. There were also baby water snakes.

If it was a very dry summer with no rain for a few weeks, the water in the creek would get very low and barely run. The mountains would be even dryer and animals and snakes would come down to the lower creek beds for water. The animals were no problem but most of the snakes were poison and everyone had to be looking around when they were outside.

A trip into the mountains surrounding our home was a wonderful assault on your sense of smell and hearing. The woods could be very noisy from the sounds of the animals scurrying, insects, birds and from far off the sound of dogs barking down in the valley. It was always cool in the woods no matter how hot it was. The ground under the trees could be hard from rocks and dry soil to a cushion step from the pine needles, rotten leaves, decaying broken branches and moss formations.

We always let our imaginations go wild. One time we would be Indians looking for food to tracking animals or we would be cowboys tracking the Indians. We stayed in the mountains until the sun started sinking low in the sky. As brave as we were in the daylight, none of us wanted to get stuck in the woods alone at night. We would eat the way the Indians did, there were lots of berries, fruit, nuts, seeds and wild plants. Water was usually easy to find too.

Every spring the mountains came alive with new growth and fragrances. A favorite past time then and now was to go to the mountains and pick wild greens as a food source. There were ramps, mustard greens and poke salad. My Mamaw Cloud loved mustard greens and poke salad with hot bacon fat poured over them with a piece of hot cornbread from the oven. There was wealth in the mountains if you were willing to walk up those hills to look for a special type leaf with small red berries and dig up their roots. I am talking about Gin Sing. My dad never had much cash money but he dug "Sang" as it was called. The roots were dried and sold, to whom I don't know but the money he got helped him to buy things that were needed.

I hope this story helps you to close your eyes and hear, smell and see the wonders I have described.

41

Our Garden

The most basic things to comfortable living in the cold winter was having enough food, warm clothing, blankets, coal and wood for the stoves.

Dad's garden was on top of the mountain on the right side of Stretchneck Holler halfway around to the next mountain formation. It was quite a hike up there. We had an old mule that was used to plow the garden in the spring. The mule was used for my father's garden and his parent's garden. The mule also hauled the sacks of corn and other vegetables on his back down the mountain to our house.

I wasn't taken up the mountain to the garden too often. I would mostly stay with Mamaw Cloud. Dad thought I should get some experience being up there with them in the garden. So my job would be to sit between the rows of corn and pull weeds. There was a spring up there and mom would bring mason jars full of milk, which she kept in the spring until we were ready to eat lunch.

One time when I was up there the mule got spooked when my older brother Roger was using him to plow. The mule pulled the rains out of Roger's hands. Daddy had to go chasing the mule all the way to the end of the garden, which was quite large. Roger had started plowing with the mule at about eight years old. I don't know who he was more scared of the mule or daddy. But my guess would be daddy.

Roger had to do the job of a grown man when he was young. He helped daddy in the garden, brought both cows down out of the hills every day for mom and Mamaw Cloud, I think mom always milked the cows. Roger had to be at daddy's beck and call at all times. Daddy was a teacher of hard knocks. He would tell you how to do something and if you didn't listen well, he would just sit back and wait for the consequences. Daddy figured you would learn better from your mistakes than from him going in to every little detail and leading you through the way to do things. Daddy was preparing Roger for the things he would need to know to make a living off the land.

Roger grew up, went off to the Navy, came back and spent a little time with Mamaw and Papaw Cloud. He went to Louisville where we were living, got a job in construction. I imagine most of the lessons learned from daddy came in handy in his life.

In August and September the vegetables from dad and Papaw Cloud's gardens would ripen and be ready to eat or preserve.

Mom and Mamaw would work at Mamaw Cloud's house. A fire would be built in the front yard near the pump. Large rocks would ring the fire high enough to sit a washtub on top of the rocks without smothering the fire. Someone had to be watching the fire and feeding the wood to keep the fire hot at all times while everyone was busing in the kitchen preparing the food for canning.

The biggest crop would always be corn, tomatoes and potatoes. Tomatoes would be placed in a large pot of hot water just until the skin split. The tomatoes would go into a bowl or onto the table for pealing. The skin comes off really easy. After peeling the tomatoes they would be quartered and placed into canning jars along with their juices. The lids and cans would have been boiling on the stove also to get them sterilized. The rings and lids would be lifted from boiling water as they were needed.

Once the lids were tightened the jars would be carried outside and put in the washing tub of boiling water and cooked for a specific amount of time. This all depended upon what was being canned. String beans only had to be blanched and added to the jars with their liquid. Tomatoes only needed their skins removed and cut into manageable parts and filled with hot water. For cucumbers, pickle relish, bread and butter pickles all that needed to be done was sliced, spices, vinegar and water were brought to a boil and the jars would be filled and the lids and rings screwed on tightly. The jars would be set on the kitchen table and would be checked later to be sure that the lids had made a popping sound and the lid would not pop up when pressed.

Green beans would be brought down off the mountain in bushel baskets or burlap sacks. The horse would bring down everything on the wooden pallet that would be ties to the shoulder harness of the horse. Beans had to have their strings removed and be broken up before they could be blanched and put through the canning process.

Green beans were also preserved in a different fashion. The strings would be removed, beans washed and then the stringing of the beans would begin. I remember my fingers being raw from doing this. A large string and needle would be handed out by Mamaw Cloud. The needle would be stuck though the middle of the green bean and the bean pushed down to the end of the string. Every time a string would be full of beans, and I would say I am done, Mamaw Cloud would push those beans down on the string as tight as she could and hand it back to me. The string would only be half full.

Once all the beans were strung they would be laid on a sheet or other old material in the sunlight, on the ground or on top of the smokehouse roof. These beans were referred to as shuck beans. When they were completely dried they would be hung up in the smokehouse or dad's barn until they were ready to be cooked and eaten.

Beets would have the ends with the leaves and roots cut off, washed and blanched. Beets were a root vegetable like potatoes, parsnips and leaks. Beets also took a long time to get done when cooking so they were boiled in the big washtub for a few hours before they were put aside for the jars to seal.

Before the invention of refrigerators with freezers, corn was eaten as it was picked. It was boiled and cut off the cob and fried in an iron skillet with lots of butter and salt until it was soft. The corn that was not eaten was left to dry out. The dried corn stalks with the corn attached would be cut down and brought off the mountain on a pallet by the mule and placed in our barn. The corn would be removed from the corn stalks and piled in a corner. The shucks were used in the past for mattress filling. The corn would be shelled off the corn into containers and saved to be ground into meal or fed to the animals.

Onions were a staple of our gardens for flavoring almost every dish made. The onions would be pulled out of the ground whole. The green stems would be tied into bunches and allowed to dry by hanging them like the beans were hung up in the barn or smoke house.

Potatoes were dug up in a quantity to last for a few days. They were mashed or fried. When you were tired of having mashed they would be fried until we got tired of them that way. Potatoes would last for a longer period of time when they were placed in a cool dry dark place like our caller. Daddy had built a dairy for storing his vegetables, fruits and canned goods. Daddy dug into the mountain. He built the left and right walls and front walls and door out of wood. The floor and back wall was of dirt. He made shelves for mom to store her jars of food. The air in the dairy was always cool. There were bins or containers for the potatoes, green tomatoes and fruit. Green tomatoes would be kept in the dairy and eventually would ripen and turn red. Pears were picked in September when they were hard. They were wrapped in newspaper and left in the dairy in a bin to ripen.

Other food stuffs were gotten in the surrounding mountains, valleys and creeks. Animals were raised for food and some animals were hunted for food. Junior Cloud loved to hunt. He always had squirrel dogs. Our meat came from hogs and chickens that we raised squirrels and rabbits that daddy shot when he went hunting.

There were numerous apple trees in the mountains and valleys in Dizney. Papaw Cloud's father and his brothers planted the fruit trees. Some of the brothers were pretty good nurserymen and had taken several different kind of apple trees and grafted two of each into one tree to produce a new variety of apple. Apples were a great staple eaten raw or cooked into apple butter, apple sauce, filling for cakes and pies.

There were also wild blackberries, raspberries, and strawberries for picking. Those that weren't cooked and made into cobblers or pies were made into jelly or canned whole for later use. The other fruit that was used for cobblers was rhubarb. The smell when cooking was terrible but it tasted pretty good.

There were numerous nut trees too. There were Beechnut, black walnut and chestnuts are all I can remember. Beechnuts were not used for any particular recipe we just ate them from the trees. Black walnuts were delicious eaten plain or added to cakes and muffins. Chestnuts were good roasted in the fire place or in the coal stove.

Black walnuts required a tremendous amount of work to even get to the point of eating them. They had to be shaken from the tree because the trees were too big to climb and pick the nuts. They were brought down out of the mountains in burlap sacks. There was a thick green hull that had to be removed before the nuts could be placed into the sun to dry out. The green hull would stain anything it got into contact with; your hands, and clothes. After they dried out the shell was so hard it had to be broken open with a hammer. Sometime they still did not just drop their juicy meat into your hand. You had to dig out the nut with a pointed object. My mom favored a hairpin. We would spend hours in the fall cracking open black walnuts and digging out the meat.

There were also greens that grew wild that kept people from starving and people of the 50's would still take a walk into the mountains and pick ramps, poke salad, mustard and turnip greens. All these were boiled or eaten raw with hot bacon or sausage fat poured over the leaves. Mamaw Cloud was partial to the latter way of eating her greens. Poke salad and ramps were boiled and eaten. Ramps had a really strong pungent smell. It smelled up the house when cooked. It made your breath stink after being eaten. Most school teachers would tell the students if they ate ramps to not come to school until the odor wore off.

No one really knows where the ramps came from. The smell had a strong garlic type smell. They grew out of the ground the same as an onion, but the green stem was flat instead of round like an onion. I would think that it evolved over the many years that it has been propagating itself. It probably came from the American Indians who lived in this region before the white settlers came.

42

Cousins and Best Friends

School always ended around the end of May and resumed the middle of August. The reason for this schedule is that children needed to be free to help with the planting of the crops and that usually was done at the middle to end of May.

Everyone waited for the end of May with such anticipation. We would be free of school and after helping with the crops we were able to do whatever we wanted to amuse ourselves for two and one half months. My Aunt Pauline's children and I and my brothers were very close. We lived at the top of the holler below Mamaw and Papaw Cloud. Pauline lived at the beginning of the holler.

We all loved the mountains and would head for the hills at any opportunity. It was cool under the trees on a hot summer day. Most of the time we could not see the sky the trees were so tall and thick. I could not imagine letting my girls go to the mountains at any age. There are rattle snakes, copper head snakes, deadly spiders, wild animals and all kinds of accidents could happen. The ground was usually soft from leaves falling in the fall, pine trees shedding their needles, rotting branches and other matter.

It was always noisy in the forest. The animals would be warning each other that we were entering their domain. The buzzing of the bees, drone of the flies, chirping of the crickets, squirrels and rabbits chatter. Most of the noise was from the birds. There were too many varieties to count. There were bluebirds, cardinals, finches, doves, pheasants, blackbirds, crows, mocking birds imitating other birds, wood peckers pecking on trees, turkeys, and hawks soaring on the wind looking for small animals to swoop down and capture for food.

The other animals in the mountains were foxes, squirrels, chipmunks, rabbits, snakes (copperheads, rattlesnakes, blue racers, black snakes, garden green snakes, etc.), possums, mountain lions, panthers, bob cats and a more. Most of the animals would not bother us. They usually would find a place to hide.

When we were preparing to go into the woods we would take along some water and some sort of sandwich. If we got hungry after the sandwich we could always look for some wild strawberries, raspberries and blackberries. We knew to keep to the mountains surrounding our holler.

We would pretend that we were explorers or Indians. Mostly these were Cherokee Indians. The trail of tears set up by the United States government to walk the Indians of the southern states to reservations in the west. I read a book about this when I was in high school and cried because of the horrible things that were done to those people. Most of these Indians died in route. The Indians in the mountains of south eastern Kentucky intermarried with the white settlers. My great grandpa Andrew Jackson Presley's mother was a full blooded Cherokee. That made me and my cousins 1/8 Cherokee. There are hieroglyphics written on rock out cropping in these hills. We discovered flints shaped into arrow heads. There were lots of clues that the Indians lived in these mountains.

We would never go over the mountain into the next valley, we were afraid of getting lost. We usually made sure we could see some of the houses in Stretch Neck or had a good idea where they were. We usually followed existing trails. If you got off the trail you could walk right off a cliff before you knew what was happening. We would encounter lots of obstacles to get around or climb over. Usually they were old broken down fences from houses long gone.

I was as tough as my brothers and as far as I was concerned no body was leaving me at home. Sometimes it was a struggle and my brothers would have to stop and wait for me. They were so used to me that no one every made the excuse that because I had polio I could not follow them anywhere. I also played follow the leader with them. That sometimes led me into trouble.

When we played Indians we would catch lightening bugs and use the light to decorate our faces with war paint. Our horses were dead tree limbs between our legs with a string tied to the end in front of us and we would gallop away. We used to play cowboys too. A favorite was Bonanza. Also we would play Wagon Train. Lanny and Roger would be the wagon masters and Tony would be the scout who rode ahead to look for any signs of Indians or bandits.

Sheila and I were more like sisters than cousins. We spent as much time together as we could. Sheila, her mom was dad's sister, and her family moved back to Dizney from Michigan when I was about seven or eight years old. Sheila, Andrea and I would play ring around the rosy. We sang lots of old children songs. We took off our starched crinoline slips and put them on our head and pretended we had long beautiful hair.

When we all got together, my brothers and her sister and brother, we usually ended up in an argument or fight. If Tony and Andrea got into a fight, then Sheila and I would end up fighting because we were each taking up for our siblings. Roger and Lanny usually just walked away and didn't get into the fracas. Mostly we played outside in the summer time.

We would go blackberry or raspberry picking. These bushes grew wild but were probably planted by someone. The way they spread and continue year after year is through birds eating the berries and their droppings landing on the soil and the seeds taking root. We used to pick them in the creek banks. We had to keep an eye out for snakes no matter where we were playing. Most snakes would rather not cross paths with humans so when they smelled or heard you coming they would leave the area or hide. The only danger was if you happened to step on one while it was snoozing in the sun or get near the den.

We played in the creek when it was real hot and we needed to cool off. There were baby fish (minnows), tad poles, crawfish and sometimes baby water snakes. The only thing you had to be careful with was the crawfish. They really hurt if they caught you with their pinchers.

The creek in Stretchneck Holler that was near my house was safe to play in because our toilets were not built next to the creek bank. It wasn't deep enough to go swimming in but you could lie down or sit down and get wet enough to cool off. Some areas you could walk right into the creek and some areas had high banks too steep to climb in or out.

In the spring when the snow melted or if we got a lot of rain at one time the rain came rushing down the mountains into the creeks. There were small bridges and round concrete cupboards along the way to the stream that ran next to the highway and eventually spilled into the Cumberland River. Sometimes there would be tree limbs, mud, rock, or boulders that were washed out of the mountain taking out the small bridges on their way or clogging up the cupboards and resulting in the water washing over the banks into the road or someone's yard.

We lived on the opposite side of the mountain from the creek so we never had to worry about getting flooded. After the rains stopped and the water returned to normal, we would look for old rocks and fossils. Many people have found fossils and petrified wood that had turned to stone. Every time I visit Harlan County to see relatives and I know that there were heavy rains, I would head for the creek to look for rocks to bring back to New Jersey with me. I have many rocks in my flower gardens from Harlan County.

Every summer there would be relatives come for visits and we would all get together at Mamaw Cloud's house or my Mamaw Hale's house depending on which side of the family it was.

Fourth of July was the best holiday. There would be lots of relatives visiting from far away places. There was lots of food, cakes, pop and ice cream. Since the Cloud's relatives mostly lived in the area, the visitors would be on Mamaw Cloud's side of the family and daddy's two brothers and their families. We could stay up the road at Mamaw and Papaw's house and play with our cousins as long as we wanted and eat as much as we were offered. Any other time daddy didn't like us to eat at Mamaw and Papaw's house. I guess food was pretty hard to come by and he didn't want us eating up their food.

One summer day when Roger was about eleven and Tony was nine, daddy took both of them to the mountains to dig for ramps. They had been gone all day and came home exhausted. Daddy wouldn't let the boys rest they had to take his great aunt a bag of the fresh ramps. They rode their bicycle out of the holler down the road past the post office and continued past Arthur Grant Pace's house. They pushed their pike up this rocky path with nothing but ruts and rocks to get to the house and deliver the ramps.

When they delivered the ramps they were too tired to walk down the steep path and both jumped on the bicycle and started riding toward the main highway. The bicycle hit a rut or rock and the front part of the frame broke. Tony was on the handlebars and he got thrown off the bike. Roger was driving and when the bike broke in half he must have landed face first on a rock and was knocked out. Tony got up off the grown to see what the matter with Roger was. Tony had cut his head and when he leaned over Roger the blood dripped onto Roger's face.

Tony ran out to the road yelling that Roger was dead. Arthur Grant, who was older than my brothers, told Tony to go home and get his mom and dad. Tony ran all the way. Dad was just at the end of Stretchneck holler when they met Arthur Grant in his father's truck. Roger was in the front seat and his bicycle was in the back bed of the truck.

Mom kept Roger from falling asleep until late that night. When Roger finally fell asleep mom stayed up with him. Mom woke him up ever so often to make sure he was still alive. A head injury was supposed to be very dangerous if the injured person fell asleep too soon.

When Roger was around twelve years old he stepped on a nail. Mamaw Cloud made different kinds of poultices to put on his foot. She had a number of recipes that was supposed to draw out the poison.

Luckily mom gave up on Mamaw Cloud's poultices after a couple of days and took Roger to the Harlan Hospital. The doctor said Roger was very close to getting lock jaw. He was given a few medications that did not improve his condition. The last thing that was given to him was a thick medication in a syringe and needle. The doctor told mom that he hated to have to give this medication to a child Roger's age since it was hard on an adult. He gave Roger the shot of medication and mom said Roger never showed any outward emotions of pain except that big tears rolled down his cheeks.

Roger was released from the hospital in a few days and was lucky to be alive. Tony never had any major accidents that I can remember. Donnie was too small to get into much trouble.

Sheila and I would climb the wagon trail up to the flat area where the cows grazed. We would play house in an unusual way. We would collect rocks and make a picture on the ground with the rocks outlining rooms of a house. We made dolls from sticks or pretended they were dolls. We would play house for awhile and then we would play Indian princesses. We were as close as any sisters could get. I missed her something terrible when we moved to Louisville.

43

Church on Sunday

In order to tell you about our Sundays, I have to start on Saturday. Mom and Roger would bring in enough water to fill up the washtub that was for our weekly bath. A fire had to be built in the kitchen stove to warm up the water so wood and coal had to be carried into the house also. Considering all the hard work mom had to go to for us to have our bath, I understand why it was only a weekly thing.

During the week, if there was school she would make sure the parts that showed were washed before we left the house. The first person in got a clean hot bath, by the last one the water was not so hot or clean anymore. In the summer mom would open the door from the kitchen to the room that was never finished. She would put the washtub just beyond the door opening and we would have a little bit of privacy.

Sunday morning after breakfast, mom would have us all dressed and lined up for our hair to be combed. The boys had to deal with a wet comb and some kind of gel to keep their hair in place (I think.) My brothers will have a fit if I am wrong about that. Mom always starched everything from shirts to overalls. The boys hated those starched clothes. I guess sometimes they got pretty good rashes. I had the worst ordeal though. On Saturday night while my hair was still wet, Mom would take what seemed like forever to get my curly head looking just right. I would wake up with frizzy hair and cry.

So out of the holler we would go, without daddy because he never went to church after he moved out of Mamaw and Papaw's house. Just below our house there was a small cliff on the right side and a space on the other side of the road to the right where cars could turn around and the creek was just

179

behind this turning place. Next we would pass Uncle Elmer Presley's barn, his wash house and finally his house. Uncle Elmer was Mamaw Cloud's brother. Uncle Elmer went to church almost every Sunday. Aunt Maudie was sick a lot but she came to church with Uncle Elmer when she was feeling okay. Maxine, Helen, Alene and Larry went to church every Sunday. Their older brother and sisters had moved away.

Next we passed Frank and Mary Jane Cloud's house. Then we passed Homer and Jenny Cloud's home. The last house on the right was where Pauline Grubbs, my dad's sister, and her family lived.

Sometimes if we were early for church we would wait on the porch at Aunt Pauline's house until everyone was ready to go. It was a good half mile from the top of the holler to the bottom where the paved road was. Past Pauline's house the valley opened up running the opposite direction left to right. There were houses to the left and right of the creek with a large empty area in front of the "big bridge" to the highway that ran on the other side of the creek. Then we walked to the left down the road a little piece to where the church stood on the right side of the road up against the mountain side.

The church had two levels. The first level was for the Sunday school class-rooms. There was a door to enter the first level just beside the road. The entrance at the front of the church had very steep concrete steps with a concrete side going up to the front door on the second floor. There were double doors at the entrance. Only one side was opened for church service. The two doors were opened up if there was a funeral. Through the front doors there was a row of pews on each side of the middle aisle. The aisle led to the alter, which was at the back of the church which faced west towards the end of the town. To the left of the door was a stairway that led down to the first floor classrooms.

At the back of the church where the pews ended, there was a three foot area that was empty before the alter began. The alter was raised about six inches and was about twenty feet wide. On the alter was the piano and the wooden stand that held the bible for the preacher. The height of the wooden stand was maybe four and a half feet and about two feet wide. Depending on the preacher and whether he was filled with the Holy Spirit, he would walk back and forth across the alter and preach. There would be a large white handkerchief in his hand to wipe the sweat off his brow.

Behind the stage were two small rooms, one at each end of the alter. These two rooms were the classrooms of the adult men and women's bible classes. In the room on the left there were a few steps leading up to a door where you would enter the choir area. As you entered, to the immediate left next to the wall and just before the benches began were steps that led up to each row of benches until you reached the last row. The choir had about eight rows of long benches. The benches were each raised a step higher than the last one. The entire choir area was raised about two feet above the alter so that everyone in the church could see the entire choir. On the back of each bench was a small wooden area that held the song books. On the first row the song books were left on the seats after the singing was over. The rest of the benches in the church had the same songbook holders as the choir. At the back of the choir was a stain glass window. To see the sun coming through this window was a grand site.

Any member of the congregation that wanted to sing in the choir would go up to the choir when they were requested to sing, which was every Sunday morning church service before the bible classes and the reading of the minutes were read. My mom and I always sang in the choir. The church piano was played by Mrs. Lucy Pace.

After the singing there would be business announcements from the secretary as to the amount of money given earlier and the total of the money in the church's account. Any other announcements of importance would be announced, such as upcoming revivals, who was sick and needed praying for, prayer requests taken from the congregation and prayer requests for those not saved and in need of accepting Jesus as their savior. My dad had a lot of prayers said for him.

Then everyone would get up and go to their respective classrooms. Bible study was for everyone, adult or child. My favorite Sunday school teacher was daddy's mother Leona Cloud. My cousins Sheila and Alene were in my Sunday school class. The other girls were Wanda, Cleta May, Christine, Fay and probably other girls I cannot remember at this time. After the reading of the lesson from the material supplied by the Southern Baptist Conference Group, we would have a question and answer discussion period.

After Sunday school was over some of the people would leave and others would stay for the sermon which would be another hour. The people who left after Sunday school usually came back at 7:00 that night for the second sermon. Sometimes mom would stay for the early sermon and bring us back again for the evening sermon. On Wednesday there would be an evening sermon. All the churches had the same schedule for their sermons.

The sermons usually lasted from 7:00 pm until 8:00 or 8:30 pm. Of course it seemed much long to us when we were children. My brother Tony usually lay down on the bench beside mom and went to sleep. Most of the times that we walked home on Sunday nights it would already be dark. There were lots of wild animals in those mountains in the 1950s. When we walked home with one flash light we stuck together like glue. Years before the people only had a kerosene lamp to light their way outside and inside their houses. I remember hearing the cry of a panther in the mountains when we were walking home in the dark. We all lined up in a row across the road so no one would be trailing behind.

Daddy used to go to Church with his family until he got married and then he stopped. Mom, however, always went to Church and would drag all of us four kids with her. I think this was how she made friends and met the people of Dizney when she and dad first got married. I can remember being in Church on Sunday nights in the hot summer. All the adults had a cardboard fan. The children fell asleep when it was very hot.

There were usually a few revivals in our church in the warmer weather. I remember one particular revival that the church had. I was so scared of some of the preachers that I would be hiding in the floor. Not all but some of the preachers were all hell fire and brimstone. They would get right up in your face and try to intimidate you into coming forward to accept Jesus as your savior. I am sure that this intimidation and fear was what persuaded some people to accept the Lord. Other times the revivals would get the older folks to shouting all over the place and the kids had no idea what was going on. My Mamaw Cloud used to do a lot of shouting. Adults just did not explain things to children back then.

For those who don't understand I believe shouting is when your heart gets so overjoyed when you have the spirit of the Lord entering your mind and sole. I never had that experience in Church, even though I was baptized in the creek when I was about ten years old. My family moved away after I turned thirteen. I am sure I would have gotten stronger in my faith if we had not moved to Louisville, Kentucky. The ten years that we lived in Louisville we never found a church that we felt comfortable in. I did go with my girl friend to her church and liked it a lot. I only got to go to her church when I was able to sleep over at her house as she lived in a different area than I did.

The closest I got to being filled with the Holy Spirit was in a Church Auditorium in Ocean Grove, New Jersey. This auditorium dates back to the early 1800s. My husband and I were there to see a concert by the Christian group "Blind Boys of Alabama". Their songs got this very conservative crowd on its feet, me included. The Lord was definitely at that gathering.

In the summer the church would have a week for vacation bible school for all the children. We would be told bible stories and have lots of crafts and pictures to color.

Each Sunday after mid-day services the pastor, if he did not live in the area, would be invited to dinner and the afternoon visiting with a different family each week. Daddy really hated it when mom invited the preacher to dinner. He had to be on his best behavior and only hope that the preacher did not try preaching to him and trying to convert him.

Mom would clean the house for a week before the Sunday she would be having the pastor for Sunday dinner. She would kill the best chicken in our chicken lot and cook some of her best recipes. It wouldn't matter to us that the preacher was visiting we were always on our best behavior because mom and dad were very strict. We would be outside playing until it was time to eat and then back outside we would go to play. We had to stay as clean as possible so that when it was time to go back to church for the Sunday night service all we had to do was put on our clothes that we wore to the morning service.

On regular Sundays we would go back up Stretchneck Holler. Mom would kill a chicken and fry it for dinner along with cornbread, green beans, mashed potatoes, fried okra or green tomatoes. The best Sunday meals would be in the summer when we had fresh produce. We had a cow so we always had fresh milk and butter. Honey was our sweetener as sugar was too expensive.

Some Sundays mom's sister would pick us up and take us to mom's parents house about three miles away. Mom would make sure that she had cooked a meal for dad and he only had to heat it up when he got hungry.

44

School Days

In the first grade mom would take me out of the holler every day for school. She got the school bus to pick me up and drop me off at the bridge at Stretch Neck Holler.

My left leg was weak from the Polio I contracted in 1949 at 11 months old. Mom would hold my hand so I would not fall if my leg got tired and gave way on me. All my life I have had to hold my left leg just above my knee because when the muscles in the leg got tired they could not hold my knee in a locked position and my knee would buckle and I would fall.

That first winter of school, when the holler got hard to travel from snow and ice mom would keep me home from school. I missed half that first school year but my teacher passed me to the second grade. I did not have any problems with keeping up with the second grade lessons the following fall.

As I got older and my polio leg became stronger from the walking in and out of the holler I no longer needed mom to walk me out of the holler, unless it was snowing or sleeting. After a few years I would walk out of the holler for school with my brothers and I started walking to Jones store to wait for the bus. The bus kept dropping me off at the big bridge after school though.

At Jones store the other children, my cousins Sheila and her brothers and sisters would sometimes buy a small cake, peanuts or candy for lunch. Sometimes we would charge one thing extra to go with our sandwich if mom didn't have the nickel to give to us. Almost everyone in Dizney had a credit tab at Jones store. I loved to get a bottle of RC pop with a bag of peanuts. I would pour the peanuts into the soda, and the peanuts tasted so good as you drank the soda and ate the peanuts.

When the school bus picked us up at Jones' store we went past the church on the left and the creek was always on the right side of the road. There was no room for houses on the left side after we passed the church. On the other side of the creek were a few houses and then the big bridge leading across the creek to Stretchneck holler. As the bus continued on down the road the mountain continued to be to the immediate right of the road and the creek to the left of the road. There were houses along the wide area on the other side of the creek once we passed the big bridge at Stretchneck holler. These houses were not close to each other and as we drove along there would be foot bridges leading over the creek to the different houses. Behind all of these houses the mountain would rise into the air several hundred feet high. All the mountains in this valley town rose several hundred feet. There was another larger bridge for cars to pass over at Yokum Creek holler just before the school grounds began. The school yard and school were on the right side of the road. The bus would stop in front of the school and let the children off. Then the bus would travel a few feet farther down the road to a wide area where the road ended, the bus had room to turn around and Turners creek holler began.

The Dizney grade school building was in the shape of a horse shoe. The building faced the county road. There was a covered porch that ran from one side around to the other end on the inside of the building. There were two sets of steps going from the ground to the porch on each side of the porch. The porch did not have a railing. There was a large area in the middle of the building that was dirt and weeds. Some of the children played in this area at recess. The bigger children played in the larger area of the school yard to the left of the building along the road. The creek that we followed along the road to the school house branched off at Yokum Creek holler. One tributary flowed from Yokum Creek and the other one came from behind the school grounds and up Turners Creek holler.

On rainy days or if the sun was too hot to play outside, we would sit in the shade on the porch and eat our lunch. My brothers and I usually took bologna sandwiches or peanut butter and jelly sandwiches. The bologna we got at Jones store and the peanut butter came from Aid to Dependant Children that the county gave out to the poor families.

There was no running water, in-side bathrooms or central heat. There was electricity. We had outside toilets, one for the boys and one for the girls. Each room had a potbelly coal stove. The boys would bring in coal and kindling for each room. The teachers had to get there early enough to have the fires going when the school bus dropped us off. Each room had a bucket and a dipper to drink the water. This was not very sanitary. Cold germs were easily spread. One boy in each classroom would be in charge of taking the water bucket to the pump on the school property and refilling it when it got empty or warm.

The school consisted of three rooms on the back end of the building and one large room on either side of the building. When I was going to school in this building the one room on the left side of the building was used to hold supplies. In the 30s and 40s there were a lot more families with children living in Dizney and all the rooms were used for classrooms.

Some classrooms had two or three grades in the same room. The first and second grades were in the room on the back right side of the building. The middle classroom was for the third and fourth grade. The room on the back left side was for the fifth and sixth grades. The large room on the left was used at one time for a lunch room. Food was cooked here by the teachers and sold to the children who had the money to pay. I don't believe this experiment lasted long. The food was not so great, the children from Turner's creek and Yokum Creek could walk home to eat lunch and most children brought their lunch from home. Most of the families just did not have money to spend on school lunches.

The school was supplied with all pencils, paper, books and other supplies by the county board of education. We certainly were too poor to buy school supplies such as pencils and paper ourselves. Each classroom had one entire wall from half way up used especially for the blackboards. At the bottom of the blackboards was a small piece of wood that went across the entire length that held the chalk and erasers.

The school books were used over and over each year. The only supplies that were needed each school year were paper, pencils, crayons and chalk. Art and school lessons not in the books consisted of stenciled papers. I am not sure if each teacher had their own stencil box or if one was shared by all the teachers. The box was big enough to hold standard 8 ½ by 11 inch paper and the bottom portion was filled with jell. I think the jell was blue or purple. It smelled pretty bad.

The teachers used this stencil box to make copies from a master page that was drawn or written with the special stencil pen. The teacher would place the original printed piece of paper onto the strong smelling jell and close the top. When the paper was removed the form on the original would be pressed into the jell. The teacher would place a blank piece of paper face down on the jell and the closing of the door pressed the picture into the blank piece of paper. One piece of paper would be made from the stencil box for each child in class. This was an early form of a photocopy machine.

My favorite teacher was Mrs. Cusick. She was so good to me. She took me and my friend Wanda home with her a couple of times to sleep over. We had to walk across the Cumberland River on a swinging bridge to get to her house. That was scary. Guess that's why I only slept over a couple of times. Mrs. Cusick gave my younger brother Donnie a cat. He brought it home and daddy had a fit. But mom persuaded him to let Donnie keep it.

At the time there was no separation of church and school. Religion was a very important part of our schooling. Prayer was allowed in school. There was a man who came to the school once a year just before school was out. He must have been a preacher. When he came it was like a big party. There were prizes and games for the students. One child from each class who memorized the most bible verses would get a prize from Mr. Pinky. When I had memorized a few bible verses and was confident I could say them all without making a mistake I would go to Mrs. Cusick and repeat the bible verses to her. Mrs. Cusick would keep a record in a notebook for each student who said their bible verses and present it to Mr. Pinky when he came.

The pictures of all the students gathered by the school house in the mid 1950s, was arranged by Mr. Pinky. He brought the photographer who took the picture. I assume that each family that had one or more children got a picture either free or for a small charge. Mom gave me the picture she had when I was in high school and I kept it until it fell apart. When I was making my first web page someone was nice enough to e-mail me the school picture.

Each teacher had their own special paddle and they didn't hesitate to use it. Most students who got paddled at school got another one at home just to reinforce the punishment. There weren't very many problems at school. Every now and then some boys would get into a fight at recess. No parents ever came to the school that I know of. All the teacher had to do was send home a note if something needed to be relayed to the parent.

Once a year we had another visitor that if we knew when she was coming, we all would have stayed home sick. There was never an advance warning from the teachers. Mrs. Boggs, the county nurse, would arrive with her black bags and needles once each year. The news spread like wildfire. Kids started screaming and crying as soon as they heard the news. To me she brought only pain and a dozen trips to the outside toilet. She just scared the "you know what" out of me. It's a wonder I didn't just pass out while I was waiting in line. She instilled a lifelong fear of shots and needles.

My cousin Sheila told me of her experiences with Mrs. Boggs. She didn't say she was scared. She just said that my younger brother Donnie was usually in line with her when it came time for their shots. She would try to give Donnie some comfort and courage. Donnie was a skinny little boy and he just shook all over with fear. He was among those screaming and crying when he heard that she had arrived.

Mrs. Boggs would have one of the teachers sit with her and enter the shots into each child's record form. Mrs. Boggs, as I watched her from my place in line seemed to be stabbing that needle really hard into the other children's arms. Mrs. Boggs was a very grumpy person and would not hesitate to yell at the children grab their arm and shake them if they tried to resist getting the shot. We all were very relieved to see her go.

When I was in the seventh grade at Evarts, Mrs. Boggs came there. She remembered me and said hello. She asked me if I wanted to assist her. Boy, my big chance came at last. The county now sent permission slips which the parents were to check the shots that the children needed. Mom said I have no idea what shot you need. I told mom not to worry that I knew what I needed. So, I was able to forge my shot permission slip that my mother had signed and only marked down one shot that did not require a needle. So I got a vaccination instead.

We had a very big play area. The property had to be around 3 or 4 acres. We had the usual 1950's playground equipment, swings, slide, merry go round and seesaw.

We had field trips. I remember going to the coca-cola plant and the bread plant. We got to watch the assembly machinery to see how things were packaged and shipped. Most important we got to get free food samples.

Back in the 50s we didn't really have bad winters that I can remember. But I am sure that we must have had some big snows. How did our parents know if we had school or not? I guess school was never cancelled the students who lived close by were the only ones that showed up for school.

When I was in the fifth or sixth grade someone came to the school to examine our eyes for glasses. I thought it would be neat to have glasses so I lied on the exam and got my glasses. I got headaches from wearing them but I didn't know that at the time.

In the early spring one of the wild foods that probably kept many residents from starving. This flavorful food is known as ramps. The teachers would give the warning that anyone who ate ramps should not come to school because they would be sent home. The smell on your breath would knock a mule off his feet.

There were all kinds of trouble for us to get into. We had to watch out for snakes on the grounds, and inside the toilets. A swing broke and I believe it was Avis Jones who got hurt and had to be carried home. She lived pretty close to the school. She was okay.

When I passed from the 6th grade to the 7th grade, mom arranged for me to go to school at Evarts. I went on the bus with the high school students. My brother Roger was already going to school at Black Mountain School and was in the 8th grade. This school was pretty high up from the road on the side of a mountain in Black Mountain which was about four miles from our home in Dizney. When it snowed the bus could not make it up the hill to the school and the children had to walk up to the school. Mom knew that I would never be able to walk up to the school so she made arrangements with the Board of Education to let me go to Evarts school instead. I was due to start the 8th grade at Evarts that September but I was still in the hospital recovering from an operation. My parents moved to Louisville while I was in the hospital. That was terrible not to get to say goodbye to my other relatives and friends.

DIZNEY GRAMMER SCHOOL
Mid 1930s

45

Dizney Classmates of the 1950s

Here are some of the names of the children that my brothers and I went to Dizney Grade School with:

Dennis Blevins

Brenda Blevins

Vernon Caldwell

Portia Cloud

Roger Cloud

Tony Cloud

Donnie Cloud

Larry Cloud

Doyle Cloud

Billy Cloud

Joyce Cloud

Dennis Cloud

Jerry Cloud

Sue Cloud

Sargent Cloud

Doris Cloud

Faye Cloud

Sam Cornett

Velma Cox

Kathy Cox

Edward Cox

Christine Fultz

Wanda Graves

Sheila Grubbs

Andrea Grubbs

Jack Grubbs

Sonya Grubbs

Brenda Jones

Charlotte Jones

Harold Jones

Alan Jones

Beverly Ann Jones

Coy Jones

Margaret Jones

Merrill Ann Middleton

Debbie Miracle

Teresa Miracle

Mary Lou Napier

Ann Pace

Arthur Grant Pace

Johnny Lee Pace

Jane Aubrey Pace

Worley Pace

Jess Pace

Vernon Pace

Millard Pace

Garland Pace

Verle Pace

Betty Mullins

Cleta Mae Scott

Lana Soloe

Bobby Soloe

Freddie Soloe

June Bug Steele

Wade Thomas

Johnny Thomas

Wendell Thomas

David Thompson

Harry Thompson

Ruth Thompson

Charles Ward

Roby Ward

Lanny Walls

46

Summer Fun in the Creek

There was always something to discover and enjoy while playing in the creek in Stretchneck Holler. We would go play in the creek in our shorts because we could not afford bathing suits even if they were sold locally.

The creek in Stretchneck Holler was not deep enough to swim in where me and my brothers lived and there were parts from Uncle Elmer's property down to Aunt Pauline's house that the bank was to high to get down into the creek; besides who would want to swim in areas where the toilets let out into the creek.

All the hollers in Dizney had creek beds that had been cut out of the rock bed centuries ago. The creeks fed into the much deeper and wider Yokum Creek that ran through Dizney, Kenvir, Evarts and all the other tiny hamlets along the way to the Cumberland River in Harlan.

There were many tiny fish, crawdads, minnows, tadpoles that turned into frogs, snakes, lots of different insects that fed off the water and each other. There were plants in the creeks. The fish, minnows and tadpoles ate from the insects and parasites living on the plants in the water of the creek. The water snakes ate the baby minnows. A beautiful sight that always happened around the water was the black butterflies. They were so tame that you could walk up to them and pick them up and they would not fly away.

The moss that grew on the rocks and the creek bed were very slippery. I had to be careful that I didn't slide down and break something. If the bed rock was long enough and there was no big rocks or dips, with the help of the moss we could run, and landing on our bellies or bottoms, slide through the cold water for a short distance. The moss grew because the creek had rock walls or dirt banks with tall weeds surrounding it or the bank was very high above the water and the sun did not penetrate until the sun was straight up in the sky.

On the creek banks grew a lot more weeds, berries such as wild blackberries, raspberries, and strawberries. One could go out and play anywhere in the mountain and not find it necessary to go home for lunch as each child knew what was safe to eat and what was poisonous.

Sometimes we were sent to the creek with a bucket and our job was to pick as many berries as possible so that mom or Mamaw Cloud could make a cobbler for supper. We were allowed to eat some if we wanted to.

I have never walked the entire length of the creek in Stretchneck Holler. We usually just traveled up the creek from just below our house to above where Mamaw and Papaw's house was. It was too dangerous to go further because there could be snakes lying in wait and the creek bank in some places was too high to get out of the creek in an emergency.

In the area where there were people and animals you did not see snakes very often as the noise and danger of being stepped on by the cows or mules, or bitten and torn apart by the dogs, kept the snakes away.

After a heavy rain which might last a day or too, the creek could rise to sometimes five times its normal depth. The water would be moving so fast that if you stepped into the creek you would be knocked over and swept down stream and possibly drowned. Rocks, large boulders, trees and limbs would wash down from high in the mountains in the rushing water. At the time I didn't know what a petrified rock was or cared for any fossils found in rocks washed down by the storms.

Now my favorite thing to do when I go down to Kenvir to visit my mom is to get down in the creek and look at the rocks if I know there was a bad flood during the previous winter. Even if there were no floods I would look for pretty rocks to bring back to New Jersey to put in my flower gardens.

47

Our Animals

There were always animals in our everyday life. The mule was used to plow the garden and haul heavy loads. The mule would be taken to the top of the mountain in the fall when the harvest of the garden was done. There was a rope attached to the back of the mules bridal to pull the frame that daddy had made that was dragged on the ground. The frame would be loaded with cornstalks and Roger would climb onto the pile of corn and guide the mule down out of the mountain to Papaw Cloud and our house. When my mother knew that Roger would be doing this she would pray for his safety until he got to the house safe. She was so afraid that something would scare the mule and if he took off or rose on his hind legs Roger would be thrown and killed.

There were hogs and chickens every year. The hogs had a pen on the right side of the creek beyond the washhouse and barn. Daddy had built a wood type building to keep them out of the weather and the rest of the area was fenced in so the hogs could roam around but not get loose. Tony and I used to go over to the hog pen and pet the pigs. If they were penned up and we were brave enough we would climb into their small buildings with them inside with us. The purpose for the hogs was to fatten them up for slaughter in November. The next spring daddy would go off and buy another pig to fatten up. We never got to friendly with the hogs.

Each year some hens were allowed to sit on a few eggs until they hatched so we would always have a continuing supply of chickens and eggs. Daddy had built them a wooden building off the ground with skinny tree limbs or boards for them to roost on. He also made areas for them to lay their eggs in this building. He put straw down so the eggs would not get broken. Also there was another purpose and that was so we didn't have to go all over the hill looking for eggs laid by the chickens when we need some for baking or breakfast. There was a fence of "chicken wire" around their building and an area where they could roam around.

There were wild turkeys and what everyone called baney hens. I am not sure of the proper name, they looked like small chickens with shorter feathers, but they could fly. These hens would roost in the surrounding trees. They stayed close to our home because it was where they got food.

We had cows for milk. After the cow was milked, the bucket was taken to the kitchen and the milk strained. We had milk for every meal if we wanted it. My Mamaw Cloud had a cow too and she always saved some milk for buttermilk and butter. Mom did not churn much because she could always get butter from Mamow Cloud and we did not care for buttermilk.

In our barn were two stalls. They were used when a cow or horse was sick or preparing to give birth. I guess someone would bring a bull around if daddy or Papaw wanted to mate the cow.

Daddy always had dogs. We were not allowed to pet his dogs. He kept the dogs chained to their dog house on a wire lead for exercise or they stayed confined to their dog house which had a fence surrounding the house and a small area where it could relieve itself. Daddy bought hunting dogs. He would trade a good gun or pistol for a dog any time. He had a prized hunting dog that was named "Big Red". His dog house was in the front yard with a lead that ran to within five feet of our front porch. My cousin Alene came up one day when she was about twelve and got too close to the dog lead or tried to pet the dog and she got bit on the hand. She did not come up to my house very often.

The local inbred dogs were not worth wasting a bullet to blow their brains out according to daddy. My brother and his wife were visiting my mother a few years back and found a poor starving puppy on the side of the road. They took it to mom's house and feed it for the few days they were there. They took the dog back to Indiana. People wanted to know what kind of dog breed it was. Tony just explained that it was a Harlan County inbred dog of no particular pedigree. They were like the people in the early 1800s that were basically isolated in the hollers and small hamlets of southeastern

Kentucky and married their first cousins. The dogs mated with their sisters and mothers as well as cousins and were inbred for about two hundred years.

My little brother Donnie's teacher gave him a black cat. Daddy hated cats. Don't know how mom managed to talk daddy into letting him keep the cat.

48

Our House

If you travel up Stretchneck Holler past Uncle Elmer's house you will see our house a good distance up the road on the left side of the road high on the side of the mountain. At about the middle of our house was where the yard started high above where the approximately twenty foot rock wall started. The rock wall started at this point from the dirt road below and climbed up until it was at the side of the front yard. The rock wall followed the road which was very steep, but at the top as the rock wall followed the level front yard past the house and further on about twenty or so feet, the road and mountain met. At this point there were a couple of wooden steps that lead down from the yard to the road. The purpose of the rock wall was to hold back that part of the mountain that our house sits on. Above our house the mountain keeps going straight up for a few hundred feet. The dirt road continues to climb for another ten to fifteen feet and then level out and continue a few feet and the area of the road branched out to the right before the creek where the area was wide enough for a car to turn around. Then just above were my dad's parent's house, smokehouse and barn.

Our house was built by my father. It was built on the side of the mountain above the dirt road of Stretchneck Holler. I am not sure who built the rock wall. But I would assume it was built to hold the mountain back from the dirt road many decades before our house was built. One end of the house was against the mountain and was about twelve inches off the ground. The opposite end of the house next to the beginning of the rock wall was supported by logs about 20 feet high that held the house level. Underneath the house was open all around the house. The purpose I would assume was to keep the dampness from the mountain from rotting the lumber that the house was built out of.

When the weather was warm or not too cold, and it rained, my brothers and I played under the house in the dirt. We had rocks and tiny pieces of wood as cars and drove the cars over dirt roads we made on the ground. For some reason, when I was playing underneath the house I had the bad habit of eating dirt. That caused me to get worms in my intestines. I seem to remember Tony getting a spoon full of a horrible medicine along with me. Mom gave us grape jelly in the teaspoon with the medicine to get rid of the worms, but it did not hide the horrible taste of the medicine

On the front part of the house facing up Stretchneck holler daddy had built a porch with an enclosed wall about 2 feet high across the front of the house. There was an opening in the middle of the porch where wide wooden stairs lead down to the yard. There were no railings on either side.

For as long as I could remember we had a swing on the front porch right near the front door. My Mamaw and Papaw Hale always had a swing from the time that I was a little girl. Dad's mom and dad never had a swing. I guess it was because their front porch was not very wide and a swing would not have room enough to swing anyway. There were cane bottom chairs in use by every family.

I can remember a time at night we had a fierce thunder and lightening storm in our valley. Mom and we children were standing in the doorway of the living room looking out at the storm when a bolt of lightening hit a small tree on the hill not too far from the house. I do believe that was the last time we watched a storm in the doorway. One time daddy came home drunk. He passed up the front door and the swing. When he got to the end of the porch he fell over the high end of the porch and broke his wrist.

As you come in the front door you enter the living room. Across from the front door a few feet into the room sat a small square wood and coal burning stove. The stove was a couple of feet from the bedroom wall behind it and a stove pipe went straight up to the ceiling and on up past the roof. I remember lots of cold winter months getting out of bed, dressing real quick and huddling around the stove to get warm. Mom let the fire in the stove almost die out but would somehow cover a few hot coals and they would remain till the morning to make it easier to start the fire in the stove the next morning before we woke up.

There wasn't any insulation between the wood framed walls and the inside walls. The floor was made out of planks but no insulation. The floors had linoleum rugs over the entire area of each room to try and keep the cold air out.

There were two windows in the living room which mom kept sparkling clean with a rag, vinegar and water. There were nice curtains on the windows, probably made by mom. There was a couch and a chair and an end table with a lamp. The lamp was sitting on a lovely doily that mom had made. In the mid 50s we got a small black and white television. I remember watching Lone Ranger and Roy Rogers on Saturday mornings in the winter when there were no chores to do or we were sick. It had to have been in the winter. On Sunday nights the ritual was to watch Ed Sullivan and a western; then we had to go to sleep. On Saturday nights we watched Gunsmoke after we got our weekly baths.

To the right of the living room door was mom and dad's bedroom. There was a bed and a chest. This room had two windows too. One window was facing the porch and the other one facing the mountain on the side of the room.

From the living room door, straight ahead to the left is a doorway into the other bedroom where my brothers and I slept. There was a bed where my brother Roger and Tony slept and a foldaway bed where my little brother Donnie and I slept. There was a dresser with attached mirror and a seat; also an old peddle sewing machine.

I spent many wonderful hours in this room standing at the sewing machine pushing the petal and making clothes for the only doll I ever had. I had to be about eight years old at this time. My mother also spent time teaching me how to crochet. I used to beg mom to let me iron. Sometimes she did let me.

The kitchen was behind mom and dad's bedroom and across from the living room and our bedroom. The entrance into the kitchen was entirely open except for a half wall on either side of the opening into the kitchen. The kitchen was the biggest room in the house except for the unfinished room behind the kitchen and the boys and my bedroom. Upon entering the kitchen there was a refrigerator, the kind that had a tiny compartment at the top of the inside of the refrigerator. This little box had a door that closed inside the refrigerator. This little box was supposed to keep the food extra cold inside this box.

On the wall that faced the mountain were two windows that seemed to have been put in sideways because they were shorter and wider than the other windows. The windows were higher up on the wall also. I believe the windows opened outward towards the mountain to cool off the room. Under the windows sat the table and chairs. At the end of the room past the table was a big wood and coal burning cook stove against the wall facing the back of the house. There was a dry sink on the inside wall. We had to get our water from the pump in Mamaw and Papaw Cloud's yard. We did not have a pump or indoor plumbing. The water from the dry sink ran down a pipe to the side of the hill above the road.

Next to the stove was a door that opened up to another large unfinished room that ran the entire length of the house from the side of the mountain to the other end near the rock wall and road. I can remember this room being used for a lot of different things.

When I was very small I remember there being lots of people, Cloud cousins probably in this room. There were piles of corn and it was being shucked by some and corn shelled off the cob by others. The corn that was left to dry on the cob was used for the cow, mule and pigs. The shelled corn was ground by daddy's homemade grist mill into corn meal. Cornbread was a staple in our diets.

Daddy bought a meal grinder and an old car. He hooked the car up to one end of the barn and the motor from the car to the grinder sat near a small window just inside the barn. This was how he made extra money grinding other people's corn and ours. Also everyone probably got together to string beans on a piece of yarn or heavy thread when the harvest produced more beans than any one family could eat. The corn and beans would be shared by all who helped with the work.

We would play in this back unfinished room when we could not play outside. We used to play Frankenstein and I would climb up the sides of the walls and pull myself up onto the rafters overhead where the ceiling was never finished.

There was a door across the unfinished room from the kitchen that led out onto a small back porch. Mom used to sit out here and string her beans, peel her potatoes and apples. She would sit on a cane bottom chair with a big round aluminum pan in her lap. The strings or peals would stay in the pan and the clean vegetables would go into another bowl on the floor next to her. When the bowl in her lab was full or she was done with her work, she would stand up and throw the contents of the bowl over the porch railing down the side of the hill. Garbage was thrown out for the wild animals to eat and some garbage was burned.

Stepping off the back porch you could walk out onto the side of the mountain. I remember exploring with my brothers on the side of the mountain behind our house. We also got into some yellow jackets nests one time and I never went exploring behind the house again. You could walk around the house to the front porch because the side of the hill had been dug out far enough for two or three people to walk arm and arm behind the house.

When you walked around the back of the house you passed up the front porch and went down the hill a little ways to the front yard. If you continued on across the side of the hill, instead of going down to the yard, in the direction of Mamaw and Papaw Cloud's house you would walk past the roof of the dairy and a little further on was the most important part of our home life. Our outside toilet was far enough away from the house so that no one could smell it. Every few years a new hole was dug and the toilet was moved a few feet away. The old hole was covered with dirt.

When using the toilet in the summer time you had to open the door and look around for wasps or other kinds of bees before stepping in and closing the door. Once inside there was a bench with a hole cut out of the middle to sit on and do your business. I remember having a sears and roebuck catalog to use for toilet paper. There were times that all we had to use was a corn cob that had been stripped of the corn. That was not the most comfortable thing to be using. I never remember having toilet paper, except at Mamaw Cloud's house after she had her bathroom built. My brothers and dad were lucky. They could pee anywhere they wanted.

Mom kept a slop jar in the house to pee in at night. When it was warm you had better get to the toilet before it got dark. Because you never knew what you would run into in the dark trying to locate the toilet. There were no outside lights of any kind. There were lots of wild animals in those hills. Anyone going out at night carried a flash light.

49

Snakes

There wasn't too much that I was afraid of in my 13 years growing up in Dizney, Kentucky, except for SNAKES. Thank goodness snakes are warm blooded animals and only come out of their den in the middle of the summer when it is very hot and dry. On those hot summer days, they are not called lazy hazy days of summer for nothing, all anyone felt like doing was relaxing in the shade or taking a nap on the porch swing.

Being vigilant about watching out for snakes was not a constant thing that was on your mind, just something in the back of your mind. Making a lot of noise all the time was natural for children to do. Snakes tend to slide away from noise or lots of motion. They are smart enough to stay out of the way of cow hooves, pigs, mules, dogs and human beings in all age groups. Some times we would come upon snakes though. We knew to back up very slowly and run from the snake. We would tell an adult who would find the snake and shoot it.

The first experience I had with a snake was when I was about five or six years old. I was on the other side of the creek from our house playing when my brothers who were on the road playing saw a big snake in the creek. The snake was scary enough just to be seen. My brothers started yelling for me to run that there was a snake in the creek. To get away I would have to run across the footbridge to get to the road and then our house on the hill.

When I heard snake, I froze. I could not move or speak a word. Finally dad came running with his pistol. By that time the snake was climbing up the bank on the side of the creek where I was standing frozen like Lot's wife. Daddy ran across the bridge and pushed me towards the bridge. I instantly sprinted across the bridge and up the hill to the road. Daddy, who was my hero, shot the snake. All was well.

There were two deadly snakes in the mountains of Dizney and they were copperheads and rattlesnakes. Rattlesnakes would give you a warning by the shake of the rattlers on the end of their tails. There were several different colors of non-poisonous snakes. There were black snakes, green snake, brown snakes, blue racer and water snakes. Black snakes came in lots of sizes. Of course there were baby sizes, medium sizes and the largest ones that could be up to six foot long and large enough to swallow rabbits and squirrels whole.

On a beautiful summer day I left my house to visit my Mamaw Cloud, dad's mother, she only lived a few yards above our house. This day I decided to climb up the hill and go in through the back door instead of walking farther up the road to their front door. A small concrete slab was poured at the entrance of the back door. All houses in Stretchneck holler were built on the side of the mountain. I had to climb even higher to get to the concrete slab.

As I was nearing the slab I reached up to get a grip to pull myself up and I put my hand on the body of a snake, a very fat snake. I glanced over and saw a big blacksnake relaxing on the concrete; my reaction was to recoil in terror. That meant I had to let go of the snake and when I did I fell backwards and rolled back down the hill. That was alright by me because I could not run fast anyway and my rolling down the hill got me down very close to the dirt road in a flash. I managed to crawl to the road and walk as fast as I could get to my house.

When ever my brothers and/or cousins and I went out playing and we were going anywhere there might be snakes someone would have a stick. Usually there was a leader and the rest of us followed. The leader would have the stick and slap the brush or ground with the stick. This would scare the snakes away. Snakes cannot see but they know when danger is near by the sense of smell and the vibrations they can feel.

On one of my visits to see my parents in the 1980s my dad and I would always find things to do together to bond and talk. This one time he said lets go up to the apple orchard and get some apples. The apple orchard was almost at the top of the mountain in Stretch neck holler. The apple orchard was pretty far past dad's parent's house.

We walked up a dirt wagon rutted road past what used to be Papaw Cloud's corn field. We crossed the creek at a wide area behind the corn field. The creek was not very deed and you could step from one rock to another without getting your shoes wet. Then we followed another wagon rutted dirt road that went up the side of the mountain on the other side of the creek. The road was not straight up the hill but ran along the side of the hill at a constant rise until we got up to another flat area.

This flat area was where the cows and mules grazed at one time or another. Across from where we came up to the flat area a few hundred feet was another wagon rutted road that went in the opposite direction as the previous one. That trail was the same as before it was dug out of the side of the mountain and grew steadily high and higher until we got to another fairly level area. This wagon trail was much steeper than the other one. Mountains are a series of climbs that level off and become vertical climbs again.

This was where my great grandfather's brothers lived in the late 1800s and early 1900s. They were good nurserymen. They planted most of the fruit trees in the mountains surrounding Stretch Neck Holler. The climb to one of the big apple trees was straight up and daddy had to help me. Daddy had his usual walking stick that he took with him to the mountains. Under the apple tree that spanned about 20 feet there was only short weeds and grass with apples laying all around. Outside the circle of the tree limbs was tall weeds about four feet high.

I was slowly picking up apples and moving up the hill under the tree closer to the tall grass and daddy said "Come back down this way Portia." I asked why because I was always a curious person. Dad said, "Because you don't know when there are snakes lying in the weeds. I moved back down the incline closer to the base of the tree. Daddy was on the right side of the tree with me to the left and just a little below him when a rustling noise came from the tall weeds to the right of daddy. In a flash of reflex daddy swung out his stick and hit the largest black snake I had ever seen in the head. The snake turned and went up the hill and into the tall weeds.

I had my usual reaction. My legs turned to water, heart racing and I couldn't move. As soon as I could move I said "okay daddy, lets get out of here". His answer was "We don't have enough apples yet." I didn't wait for Daddy; I started scooting down the hill on my rear end as fast as I could go. Needless to say on my next trips to visit mom and dad I did not take daddy up on his invitations to go to the apple orchard.

The one way I could feel safe to watch snakes was when I would lay down on the footbridges over the creeks and watch water snakes swim around in the water. These snakes weren't poisonous and I was fascinated as long as they couldn't get to me.

Daddy was always the snake hunter. He never left the house without a pistol in his pocket. He always said he never knew when he would come upon a snake, whether it was close to our house or in the mountains. Also, when he went to the mountains by himself he never knew when he would run upon a two legged snake that might put his life in danger.

The only person I knew that almost died of a poisonous snake bit was my cousin Larry Presley. He went with some members of the holiness church down south to Georgia or one of those states to a big revival. Larry decided he would prove his trust in the Jesus by handling a poisonous snake. Unfortunately he was bitten and had to be driven home by some of the church members. I still don't understand why he wasn't taken to the hospital where he was bitten. Larry lived through it all but his kidneys were damaged.

The holiness religion believed in handling poisonous snakes. They are one of the many sides of life in the Appalachian Mountains. I have been to church with a cousin, Velma Cox. Velma belonged to the Church of God in Dizney. No snakes were out. I particularly enjoyed the music because they played guitars and other instruments besides the normal piano at our church.

50

Growing up with Polio

I was born on September 17, 1948, eleven months later as I was just beginning to walk, I became ill. I ran a high fever and became so weak I could not stand or sit by myself. Little did my parents know that I had breathed the polio virus into my mouth and/or nose. No one knew exactly how the virus spread or in what way it affected different parts of the victim's body. When I was an adult there was a documentary on television that explained just how the virus attacked part of the brain that controlled motor functions and nerves. My brain that controlled my nerves, muscles and motor skill from my left hip to my toes had been damaged. I would imagine the fever eventually disappeared.

Mom took me to see a Dr. Sargent who diagnosed an ear infection that would explain the dizziness he thought was keeping me from sitting and walking. A prescription was written for me but after several days I was not getting any better. I was taken to another doctor who examined me and could not get a reflex response from my left leg when he used a little hammer. He diagnosed Polio.

My mother (Irene Cloud) took me to the Harlan County Health Department to get help for me. The Health Department contacted the Shriners in Louisville, Ky. They arranged for a visit to the clinic at the Kozair Children's Hospital in Louisville, Ky. The Shriners paid for our train and bus fair for the following ten years from Harlan, Kentucky to Kosair Hospital in Louisville, Kentucky.

My first visit was about six months after I first became sick. I was put in a brace with a special shoe attached to it. The brace went up to my waist and secured there and at the knee. I was able to walk again. The brace rusted from my leaking diapers and my shoe partially rotted out. My mother said that I had to wear this brace for a few years until I had my first surgery at five years old. This operation was to correct the inadequate flow of blood in my left leg that was afflicted by polio. After the surgery I got a new brace with a shoe. The brace only went to just below my knee. This happened in 1954.

This was the first of several operations at Kozair Hospital in Louisville, Kentucky. I remember being in a ward with other children. When the lights were turned out there was a lot of crying and I was among them because I did not know where my mommy was.

There were no explanations given to children when something this traumatic was happening. Children were to be seen and not heard. When I woke up the next morning I was taken to the operating area. Ether was the choice at that time for putting patients to sleep and keeping the patient asleep. The mask scared me. The smell was horrible and my ears roared like a freight train was running through my head.

Recovery and the time I spent at Kosair Hospital this first time is a blur instead of a memory. The only memory is of being on a little outside patio play area with other children. I looked up to see mom standing in the doorway. She looked so beautiful. Her hair was combed nice, her dress was nice and she had bright red lip stick on her lips. I never forgot the color or smell of that lipstick.

After that we would travel by greyhound bus from Harlan, Kentucky to Corbin and by train to Louisville to see the doctors at the Kosair Children's Hospital clinic. We would stay with a family who mom had lived with just below Evarts, Kentucky from age 9 to 15.

William Hale's family were middle class and had a beautiful Cape Cod home in Louisville with fenced back yard and a concrete front porch with a swing. Their granddaughter Patricia Sue and I became fast friends. I slept with Patricia Sue in her beautiful room. Patricia Sue had lots of dolls, a doll house and other toys. All I had was one doll.

The next surgery was the summer before my 8th birthday. I had fallen off the top railing of our fenced in chicken lot a few weeks before and broken my arm. When I was admitted to Kosair Hospital they could not operate on me until my cast came off. Mom could not stay the entire time I was in the hospital so before the surgery she went back home to take care of my brothers and dad. My hospital stay lasted six weeks.

I was without my mom for about five weeks. I had my first dental visit then. I had never heard of or seen a dentist. There were people looking in my mouth and poking at my teeth and then they pulled one of my teeth. I only know that I was very scared and upset and swore never to let a dentist touch me again.

The day of surgery was worse than the dentist though. I fought for my life in that dentist seat and when that horrible mask was brought out again in the operating room it took several nurses and doctors to hold me down.

Mr. and Mrs. Hale, this was the family that mom lived with from the time she was nine until she was fifteen, and Patricia Sue's mother Weida would come to visit me. Daddy's aunt Octavia and two of her children would visit me too. The presents they brought cheered me up.

Once again I was in a big ward with lots of other girls. I made a friend in the ward I was in. Her name was Portia also. The food tasted great and was different from my diet of pinto beans, fried potatoes and cornbread at home. I loved every meal that was served each day.

The next surgery happened when I was 10 years old. The operation was on my left foot. I did not have any muscles to be able to lift my toes up when I made a step. The brace I had been wearing did this for me. By this time I was a pro at being in the operating room. This time I was ready for the mask and foul smelling Ether. But, thank God for progress, a needle in my right arm supplied the sleeping medication. I talked to the doctor and the nurses until I fell asleep.

I woke up screaming from pain. My mom was sick with a migraine and that was just too much for her to take, my screaming in pain that is, she yelled for the nurse and fainted. She was taken to the waiting room and they called my surgeon for help. He teased mom when she woke up for being such a bad patient, when I had been so brave in the operating room. The pain lasted for days. I would cry for a pain shot long before the 4 hours between shots was up.

As an adult I sprained my ankle requiring an x-ray of my polio foot. I told the doctor the story my mother had been told, the surgery I had as a child resulted in muscles and tendons being sewn together to make my foot permanently stiff so I would not drag my toes anymore. The foot doctor informed me that was not what was done to me. The bones of my ankle were fused together. Well, I thought, "no wonder it hurt so bad".

On the weekends a lot of people would come to visit the children at Kosair Hospital. Mom said the mayor of Louisville would come to the hospital and bring people to entertain the children. I remember people making animals and things out of balloons and giving them to us. My mother also said there were occasions when celebrities would visit the hospital. She particularly remembered Liberace. The children would be pushed into this large room in wheel chairs and beds to see the entertainers.

In the summer was when I usually had my operations and we would go to the clinic for the doctors to see how I was progressing and plan the next surgery. It was an all day affair whenever we visited the clinic. Sometimes I would have x-rays done while I was at the clinic. We would have to sign in when we got to the clinic and sit for hours until it was our turn to see the doctors. There were vending machines where mom and I got sodas and some snacks.

When my name was called we were lead to a section of this big room which had curtains around the examination tables. One thing I hated was the way I was totally ignored and the doctors and mom discussed the next surgery in their strategy to help me be self sufficient into adulthood. Some times I could not help but feel sorry for myself. One time as the doctors and mom talked I just cried with out any sound. The tears rolled down and filled up my ears and continued on down my neck. The doctor teased me by saying Portia has tears in her ears.

I developed a terrible fear of needles from my experiences in the Kosair Children's Hospital and from Mrs. Boggs the school nurse. I received my first flu shot when I was in Kosair for one of my operations. It was very painful. I never got another flu shot until I was an adult and I still had this fear that it would be as painful as when I received one as a child. Of course it wasn't and I was pleasantly surprised. Also as an adult I had to be brave when I first took my older daughter to the dentist. I had a terrible fear of the dentist because of Kosair Hospital had a mandatory dentist visit every time a child stayed in the hospital. They began going to the dentist at about three years old. This was the hardest thing I have ever done in my life was to not let the girls see my fear at just being in the dentist office.

There were children in many different conditions of disability from contracting the polio virus. I remember seeing girls and boys on lung machines. Some of their beds were in the middle of a big round metal contraption and it would roll them from a lying position to a veridical position. I did not understand what I was seeing at the time.

Some children had crooked spines and had surgeries to straighten their spines. After surgery they would have a cast from their waist to their shoulders with holes for their arms. Their heads needed to remain stationary until their backs healed. There were two medal rods attached to the front of their cast and two attached to the back of their cast. Another piece of metal was bent into a circle and attached to the four metal posts that were into the body cast. On either side of the head were two long screws that went into their scull just behind their ears. I lost my self pity in a hurry after seeing these kids with their halo casts. I really felt sorry for those children. I always considered myself lucky that I was not affected any worse than I was by the polio virus.

I will never forget the Occupational Therapist that taught the boys and girls how to make things for fun and to get their minds off the ordeal of being in a hospital. Her name was Diane Fossey. She was beautiful and I liked her a lot. I remember learning how to make pot holders, small pocketbooks and I am sure there were other projects that I cannot remember.

One of the summers I was there Ms. Fossey was all excited about her upcoming vacation to Africa. Little pitchers have big ears and I am sure she must have been talking to some of the nurses and aids. She never came back to Kozair. She is the same lady who fell in love with the gorillas in Africa and studied their habits for years until her mysterious death in the 1980s. I did not connect the lady with my Occupational Therapist until I picked up a magazine in a store in New Jersey and her picture was on the front page with a story of her life and death at the hands of poachers in Africa.

Ms. Fossey entered a contest with a local radio station to win a party that was to be given by the radio station. She won the contest and the radio station came to the hospital and gave us a party with music, games and food. That was a very special time for me. I discovered rock & roll from listening to the songs they played on the radio station while I was in the hospital and from watching American Bandstand.

The next surgery I had at Kozair was when I was 11 years old. My doctors were Dr. Fisher and Dr. Zoller. Mom thought the world of them because they were helping me so much. Metal staples were put on either side of my good knee to stop the growth of that leg so that my polio leg could grow and catch up in length so that I would not have to have a two inch buildup on the bottom of the brace.

This surgery was not so bad and I enjoyed the time I was in the hospital. I did not appreciate having to visit the dentist again. I was held down while they drilled out the cavities in my front teeth. There was no nova cane at that time and you could feel the heat from the drill along with the pain and horrible smell.

There was a girl there who went to visit the dentist and came back in only a few minutes to announce to the other children and me that the dentist said she had perfect teeth and didn't need to have anything done. I don't know about the other children, but there was instant hate for her by me.

When I was released from the hospital for one of my earlier surgeries there was a big celebration taking place on the grounds of the Hospital. There was a fish fry. I do believe this was a fundraiser. I was on crutches and had a cast on my leg. Mom and I had something to eat and walked around the grounds for awhile before catching the bus back to Mr. and Mrs. Hale's house, the people we stayed with every time we had to come to Louisville for a clinic visit or operation. Mom said people began to stop us and offer me money and by the time we left on the bus I had enough money for mom to buy me a new winter coat that fall.

The last surgery I had was to remove the staples from my knee because my legs were equal in length. My family moved to Louisville while I was in the hospital. When I was 14 the hospital contacted mom and asked if I could be on the Shriner's float in the Kentucky Derby parade. My mom was thrilled. I remember walking to the Shriner's building with mom and dad. Then I was driven in a big car to the parade staging area. Riding on the float was exciting and was the first time I wasn't overcome by shyness at so many people looking at me on the float. Mom took this picture as we passed by where my family was standing viewing the parade. Mom was so proud of me.

51

My Vulnerabilities

The thing that hurt the most growing up in the mountains of Kentucky, and probably would have happened no matter where I grew up, but because all the people in this small town were related in some way and everyone knew each other and watched out for each other's children, it hurt when I was called names and teased by the other children.

I am sure that I was a bit spoiled and no angel either. When the other children called me crip, gimp and names referring to my polio it really hurt my feelings. I was a stubborn and strong willed child and did everything possible to show everyone I was not hurt by the name calling and was no different than anyone else. I did such a good job that I even forgot there was anything handicapped about me.

I had to keep up with my brothers and cousins if I wanted them to play with me. My brothers tried hard to not make any difference between them and me. There was that one exception though. Sheila and I were best friends, cousins and thought of ourselves as sisters. Like all close family members we had our fights. I was a skinny little kid and Sheila was on the hefty side. Whenever we fought I would get the short end of the stick and my brother Tony would always step in to lend a hand to defend me. That only caused Sheila's sister Andrea or Lanny to come to her rescue. The result was that we all would end up fighting.

There wasn't anything I wouldn't try to do just to keep up with my brothers and cousins. I followed them everywhere they went. Sometimes the boys got tired of me following them and they would avoid me at all costs.

Even though by forgetting I had a weak leg and wanting to try everything everyone else did caused me to have a lot of injuries and accidents. There were the usual scrapped knees and elbows. This didn't bother me at all. I just tried not to let mom or dad see my injuries or complain about them.

It was the other major injuries that couldn't be avoided; the broken arms and the cuts that were too large for me to hide, and my falling off the steps and cutting my head open and almost bleeding to death.

The only person who treated me "special" and I didn't get mad or upset at him was my Papaw Hale. I was his special granddaughter for a long time and he did not hold back any affection when I was at his house to visit. Mom's family was more physically loving than daddy's family, so there I could let go and be vulnerable. Except for Mamaw Hale, she never hugged anyone that I ever saw or said anything kind and complimentary either.

I had to wear a brace until I was about 14. I used to beg mom to let me go barefoot in the warm weather. When she had the money, from selling eggs, butter and milk she would buy me a pair of cheap sneakers. Since my polio foot was smaller than my good foot mom would put rolled up newspaper in the toe of that sneaker to make it fit better. Those sneakers would only last the summer because I was constantly on the go.

The one thing I hated more than the names that the other kids called me was for anyone to stare at me. I didn't want to be reminded that I was different when I caught someone looking at me. I couldn't avoid the stares because I limped when I walked and had a brace on my leg.

I grew up with terrible hang-ups and complexes about my affliction. The only way I was able to come to terms with it was when I started writing stories about growing up in Dizney, Kentucky almost fifteen years ago. When you look back on your life, the bad things always stand out in your memory and it is the ordinary day to day or uneventful things that are so hard to recall. But some of those memories will come sneaking into my thoughts as I am writing about something else.

52

Kenvir, Kentucky

Kenvir was named by taking the first three letters of Kentucky and Virginia. This town was founded by Peabody Coal Company in 1918. This operation was owned by The Black Mountain Corporation until 1953 when the name changed back to Peabody Coal Company. By 1956 the mines were closed and the coal mines were abandoned. That also left the railroad tracks abandoned.

In 1918 the roads leading from Evarts to Dizney were nothing more than wagon, horse and Indian trails. By 1922 the railroad was extended to Kenvir and a booming industry began.

The coal company began constructing homes and businesses. There were two main camps. The Number One Camp in Black Mountain where all the businesses were built and Number Two Camp in Brittains Creek. The black workers had their own separate camp known as "Colored Camp" which was between Black Mountain, just past the Red Store) and Kenvir. Official Holler was where all the officials of the mine company lived.

The Black Mountain Camp had a post office, commissary, restaurant, police station, theater, hospital, Clubhouse and drugstore. There were several boarding houses in both camps which mostly were for the single men and couples without children to live.

The hospital in Black Mountain was the one thing that was appreciated most of all by the miners and their families. The coal company charged a few dollars a month for the family insurance. Any time spent in the hospital was covered by the Miner's welfare insurance coverage.

The 1930s and 40s were a swinging time in Black Mountain. Movie celebrities came into Black Mountain to promote their movies. The most recent movies were shown at the theatre.

53

Umwa List—Local Union #6659 —Mine # 31 Kenvir, Ky

MACK A. ABT

CLIFFORD ADAMS

PLEAS ALLEN

HARRY J. ALTICE

GRSEN ANDERSON

J.D. ANDERSON

FLOYD ANDERSON

MONESE ANDERSON

LLOYD ANDREWS

JIM ANGEL   Dizney, Kentucky

TOM ASBURY

ROBERT ATWOOD, JR

STEVEN AYERS

RALPH BAILEY

ARNOLD BALLEW

ARTHUR BARNES

ELI BELEW

ALBERT BENSON

ROY BIRCHFIELD

PAUL T. BLANKEN

CLEMONT BLEVINS   Dizney, Kentucky

EDGAR BLEVINS   Dizney, Kentucky

JESS BLEVINS   Dizney, Kentucky

RANSOM BLEVINS   Dizney, Kentucky

WILLIAM BOWLING

WILLIAM E. BOWLING

SOL BRAY

LEONARD BROCK

CHARLES A BRYANT

GEORGE E. BUNDY

EUGENE BURESS

HENRY BURKHART

KELLY BURKHART

ALBERT CADDELL

JAMES CALWELL

MEREDITH CAMPBELL

ARTHUR CANADY

NAPOLEON M. CASTEEL

MORGON CATRON

JAMES CAUSEY

RILEY CAUSEY

PARIS CHARLES JR

ELDEN B. CHILDERS

ALONZO CHILDRESS

RAYMOND CHUMLEY

KEITH CLARK

CHARLIE CLOUD   Dizney, Kentucky

HARRISON CLOUD	Dizney, Kentucky
HENRY F. CLOUD	Dizney, Kentucky
HOMER CLOUD	Dizney, Kentucky
JAMES B. CLOUD	Dizney, Kentucky
JESS J. CLOUD	Dizney, Kentucky
PEARL CLOUD	Dizney, Kentucky
SIMON CLOUD	Dizney, Kentucky
TILMAN T. CLOUD	Dizney, Kentucky
TILMAN T. CLOUD JR	Dizney, Kentucky
WILLIAM F. CLOUD	Dizney, Kentucky
GEORGE W. COLE	
WILLIAM COLLETT	
BURL COMPTON	
EARL COOK	
LEONARD COOK	
LOY B. COOK	
JAMES D. COLLETT	
DANIEL F. COLLINS	
FLOYD CORNELIUS	Dizney, Kentucky
HUGHES CORNELIUS	Dizney, Kentucky
JAMES CORNELIUS	Dizney, Kentucky
DENNIS CORNETT	Dizney, Kentucky
PAUL COTHERN	
CALEB COX	Dizney, Kentucky
EARL COX	Dizney, Kentucky
ERNEST COX	Dizney, Kentucky
JOHN COX	Dizney, Kentucky
PLEASANT COX	Dizney, Kentucky

LUTHER COX   Dizney, Kentucky

McKINLEY COX   Dizney, Kentucky

WINSTON COX   Dizney, Kentucky

HENRY L. CREECH

WALTER CRIDER

ROBERT CURETON

TOM DAUGHERTY

GARRETT DAUGHERTY

BILLIE V. DAVIS

COLUMBUS DAVIS

JACK DAVIS

LENIS DAVIS

ROY DAVIS

FRED DEFEVERS

WILLIAM J. DIZNEY

VIRGIL DOTSON

RALPH DOZIER

ROSCOE DOZIER

WILLIAM DOZIER

WILLIAM DRAPER

ELMER DUNCAN

JAMES DUFF   Kenvir, Kentucky

LEONARD N. DUFF   Kenvir, Kentucky

ELMER DUNCAN

EARL DURHAM

MERELEN ELDRIDGE

ROBERT ELDRIDGE

WALTER ELLIOTT

JOE EPPERSON JR

EARL D. ENGLISH

EARL M. ENGLISH

WILFRED FAGAN

JAMES FLATH

WHEELER FLEHNOR

LEE FREDERICK

CHARLES F. FLEENOR

ROBERT H. L. FLEENOR

GEORGE R. FORD

LLOYD FREEMAN   Dizney, Kentucky

ALLEN GARNER

EARL W. GARNER

McKINLEY GIBBS

CECIL F. GILBERT   Dizney, Kentucky

JOE GILBERT   Dizney, Kentucky

OSCAR GILBERT   Dizney, Kentucky

SYLVAN GILBERT   Dizney, Kentucky

ARTHUR GILLIAM

BALLARD GILLIAM

ARTHUR B. GREEN

RICHARD GREEN

VERLIN GREEN

CHARLES GREER

JAMES G. GRIFFIN

WENDELL GRIFFITH

LUTHER GROSS

JULIUS M. GUTHRIE

LOUIS GUTHRIE

MELVIN GUTHRIE

GEORGE HAGER

JAMES W. HALE   Kenvir, Kentucky

WILLIAM F. HALE   Kenvir, Kentucky

LEE HAMBLIN

CHARLES T. HAMMACK

CHARLES HAMPTON

DREW B. HAMPTON

HAYES HARP   Dizney, Kentucky

WILLIAM R. HARP   Dizney, Kentucky

ALBERT HARRIS

BERGER HARRIS

EMMITT HARRIS

HOWARD HARRIS

VERNON HARRIS

ERWIN HATMAKER

ROBERT HATMAKER

CHARLES HAYNES

ED HELTON

BERRT HEMBLEY

BEN HENSLEY

DAVE HENSLEY

HOMER HENSLEY

MILBURN HENSLEY

PETE HENSLEY

ROSCOE HENSLEY

SAM HENSLEY

WILLIAM HOGSTON

JAMES LEE HOLMAN

LOUIE HOLOSKY

OSCAR HOLT

NEWT HOWARD

SAM HOWARD

ROBERT HUBBARD

ORVILLE HUDSON

OTIS HUFF

JESSIE HUGHES

JOHN D. HUGHES

ARTHUR HUSKEY

JESSE B. HUSKEY

ROBERT HUSKEY

ROBERT JACKSON

STERLING JEFFERS

EMMITT JESSIE

WILLIE R. JESSEE

CHARLES JOHNSON JR

FLOYD S. JOHNSON

LUTHER JOHNSON

ROY JOHNSON

THEODORE JOHNSON

BURGAN JONES   Dizney, Kentucky

CARLO JONES   Dizney, Kentucky

CHARLES JONES   Dizney, Kentucky

CECIL JONES   Dizney, Kentucky

CHESTER JONES   Dizney, Kentucky

DAVID JONES   Dizney, Kentucky

ERLEY E. JONES   Dizney, Kentucky

HENRY A. JONES   Dizney, Kentucky

JOHN R. JONES   Dizney, Kentucky

LAWRENCE JONES   Dizney, Kentucky

MARION JONES   Dizney, Kentucky

SAM JONES   Dizney, Kentucky

WALTER JONES   Dizney, Kentucky

WASH JONES   Dizney, Kentucky

ROY JORDAN

JERRY JUMP

JOHN KIDD

ANCIL KING

ASHER KING

CHAD KING

CLIFFORD A. KING

ELIJAH KING

EMMETT KING

JAMES KING

CHARLES KIRKENDALL

ALFRED E. LAMB
WILLIAM C. LAMB
JOHN I LANE
CLARENCE LAWSON
WILLIAM J. LAWSON
OSCAR LAY
WILLIAM LEACH
CHARLIE LEDINGTON
FELIX LEE
WILLIAM H. LEE
CHARLES LEFEVERS JR
WILLIAM LEGER
WILLIAM P. LEGER
ARTHUR LEITCH
JAMES LEITCH
HOWARD H. LEWIS
JAMES E. LEWIS
JAKE LEWIS
JOHN LUBERA

ELIJA (LIDGE) MADDEN	Dizney, Kentucky
GEORGE MADDEN	Dizney, Kentucky
GEORGE R. MADDEN	Dizney, Kentucky
GRANT MADDEN	Dizney, Kentucky
HARRISON MADDEN	Dizney, Kentucky
LEROY MADDEN	Dizney, Kentucky
WILSON MADDEN	Dizney, Kentucky

HUBERT MADEWELL

FONZIE MAHAN

CHARLES MARINO

MITCHELL MARLOWE

T. KELLEY MARLOWE

WILLIAM MARSH

ELMER MARTIN

JENNINGS MARTIN

JERRY MARTIN

VENUS McCOY

JAMES McCREARY

ROBERT McCREARY

ARTHUR McFARLAND

ELBERT McGHEE

ROBERT McKAMEY

EDWARD WM. McNABB

GRADY McNABB

VARDY L. McPEEK JR

PETERO MELZONI

SAM MIDDLETON   Dizney, Kentucky

ROOSEVELT MIDDLETON   Dizney, Kentucky

WILLIAM MIDDLETON   Dizney, Kentucky

EARNEST MILLER

JOHN H. MILLER

JOHN W. MILLER

LLOYD MILLER

LUTHER MILLER

LUTHER S. MILLER

ULYSES MILLER

WILLIAM MILLER

JAMES R. MIRACLE   Dizney, Kentucky

MELVIN MIRACLE   Dizney, Kentucky

ROBERT MOFFETT

ROY MONROE

JACK MONTGOMERY

JOHN MONTGOMERY

NED MONTGOMERY

A. M. MOORE

EARNEST O. MOORE

JOSEPH L. MOORE

RALPH MORGAN JR

CLYDE MULKEY

CHINE MULLINS   Dizney, Kentucky

OAKLEY MULLINS   Dizney, Kentucky

TOM MULLINS   Dizney, Kentucky

JOHN H. MURRAY

FAIRBANKS NAPIER

HOWARD E. NAPIER

PERIN A. NAPIER

WILLIAM NAPIER

WILLIAM B. NAPIER

J. TOM O'ROURKE

JAMES OSBORNE

EARNEST OWENS

BEN PACE	Dizney, Kentucky
DANIEL F. PACE	Dizney, Kentucky
GEORGE W. PACE	Dizney, Kentucky
HARVEY PACE	Dizney, Kentucky
JAMES PACE	Dizney, Kentucky
JAMES PACK	Dizney, Kentucky
L. PACE	Dizney, Kentucky
ULYSSIS PACE	Dizney, Kentucky
CHARLIE PEACE	
DEWEY PEACE	
MIKE PEACE	
DAVE PENNIX	
LACY PERKINS	
LEO PETERSON	
HARRY PHILLIPS	
CHESTER POORE	
JIM POWELL	
MARSHALL POWELL	
CECIL PRESLEY	Dizney, Kentucky
CLARK PRESLEY	Dizney, Kentucky
ELMER PRESLEY	Dizney, Kentucky
GREEN PRESLEY	Dizney, Kentucky
SHELBY PRESLEY	Dizney, Kentucky
SHERMAN PRICE	

HOWARD QUILLEN

CARL RABY
MARION RAINS
BUHLEN REYNOLDS
LEONARD REYNOLDS
JAMES RICKETT
CHARLES RIGNEY
CLYDE RIGNEY

ALBERT ROARK
ASHLEY ROARK
BURNETT ROARK
BOB ROBERTS
CHARLES ROBERTS
WINT ROBERTS
BUD ROBINSON
CORDELL ROGERS
RICHARD ROSE
DALLAS RUSSELL   Dizney, Kentucky
VIRGIL RUSSELL   Dizney, Kentucky
CARL RUTH

KENER SANDERS
BURGESS SANDERS
ROBERT SAPP
CHARLES H. SAYLOR
MILT SAYLOR

FRED SCOTT

JAMES SHACKLEFORD

CARL SHARPE

WILLARD SHARPE

RAY SHELTON

HARVE SHULER

OSCAR SHUMATE

FRANK SINGO   Dizney, Kentucky

VESTAL E. SINGO   Dizney, Kentucky

BOSTON SIZEMORE   Kenvir, Kentucky

SHERMAN SIZEMORE   Kenvir, Kentucky

TROY SIZEMORE   Kenvir, Kentucky

LUTHER SLAVEY

FRED SMALL

ELMER SMALLWOOD

JAMES SMALLWOOD

MARION SMIDDY

ALFRED SMITH

CHARLES SMITH

ESTEL SMITH

GRANT SMITH

HENRY C. SMITH

HERBERT SMITH

HOYL SMITH

JOHN L. SMITH

LAWRENCE SMITH

PAUL SMITH

ROY F. SMITH

SINE SMITH

WILLARD SMITH

WILLIAM H. SMITH

ALVIN SOLOE   Dizney, Kentucky

ROBERT SOLOE   Dizney, Kentucky

GEORGE G. SOUNDERS

JAMES E. SPURLOCK

NATH STALLARD

WILLIAM STANLEY

A. W. STEELE

ALFRED STEELE

JOSEPH F. STONER

OLIVER STONER

HARVEY TACKETT

ELBERT TAYLOR

MILBURN TAYLOR

THURMAN TAYLOR

JAMES TEMPLETON

ARTHUR THOMAS   Dizney, Kentucky

CLAY THOMAS   Dizney, Kentucky

JESS THOMAS   Dizney, Kentucky

JOHN THOMAS   Dizney, Kentucky

LAWRENCE THOMAS   Dizney, Kentucky

LUTHER THOMAS   Dizney, Kentucky

PRESS THOMAS   Dizney, Kentucky

ELBERT THOMPSON

EVERETT THOMPSON

GEORGE THOMPSON

JOHNNIE THOMPSON

FLOYD TIPPETT

GROVER TIPTON

LOUIS TIPTON

ROSS TRENT

JAMES TROSPER

MARSHALL TROUTMAN

COOPER TURNER

WALTER B. TURNER

EDD TYE

HENRY VANOVER

GRANVILLE VAUGHN   Dizney, Kentucky

LANE VOWELL

HOMER L. WALDEN

FREEMAN WALLACE

DAVID WARD JR   Dizney, Kentucky

FRED WALLACE

FREEMAN WALLACE

HARRY WALLACE

HARVEY WEBB

JOHN WHEELER

DAVID H. WHITE

DAN WHORMSLEY

ROBERT F. WIDNER JR

CARL WILLIAMS

CLAUDE WILLIAMS

WILLIAM WILLIAMS

SHERMAN WILLIFORD

ARCH LEE WILSON

HUGH WILSON

MILFORD B. WILSON

LEE R. WINN

HOMER WITT

ARVEL WYNN

BURMAN WYNN

EUGENE WYNN

FLONIE WYNN

HENRY WYNN   Dizney, Kentucky

WILLARD WYNN   Dizney, Kentucky

ROBERT L. WYRICK

LLOYD YOUNG

HORACE ZORNES

54

Memories of Junior Cloud by Tony and Debbie Cloud

I asked my brother Tony and his wife Debbie for some stories they remembered about Dad. Be prepared to laugh your self silly.

One time Junior was out hunting squirrels about dusk. He shot a squirrel out of a tree, but did not see exactly where it had fallen. He went down to the tree and went around a rock that was close to the tree. There was a rattlesnake there. Junior leaned around the rock and shot the snake with his shotgun. Junior cut the snake open and there was his squirrel.

Junior was hunting with our brother Roger. Junior fell and slid down the hill on his stomach right into a nest of yellow jackets. Roger told Tony that he came running out of there like a 17 year old.

Junior was the biggest tease. When he would catch kids coming up Stretch Neck (they were probably coming to play with us kids), Junior would take out his big knife and with the dull end he would rake it across their ears and tell them he cut off their ear. He had all of the kids in Dizney scared of him and they would hide when they saw him coming.

In the late 70's when mom and dad moved back to Dizney from Louisville, Junior was having trouble with an owl getting his chickens at night. His brother Berry who lived up the road with their mother Leona Cloud, said he would call Junior if he saw the owl. In the middle of the night the phone rang. Junior jumped up and grabbed his gun and ran outside in the cold weather barefoot and in his long johns. He was freezing but looking everywhere for that thieving owl. The phone call was not from Berry, but a

240

wrong number. Irene tried to call out the door to get dad's attention but she was laughing so hard she was not able to do anything.

When Tony and Debbie were visiting Junior and Irene at their house in Brittans Creek, Junior wanted Tony to help him move some bee hives. While moving one of them, the hive shifted on them and they dropped the hive. Junior yelled, "Tony you've killed my bees." Tony and Foolish Dog very wisely took off toward the creek and stood on the bridge at a safe distance. Junior stayed there trying to put the hive upright and back together. The bees were all over him and stinging him. Some of them were going up his overalls. Just a few days later, Roger came down and dad asked him to move bee hives again. They also managed to turn another hive over. I don't think that he ever asked either one to help him with his bees again.

Dad had a dog that was called "Foolish Dog". Tony asked him one time, "What is that dog's name?" To which Junior replied, "He aint got no name." "But Dad, Tony said, you ought to give him a name." Dad replied, "He don't need a name, he knows who he is."

One time, Tony had gone groundhog hunting with Junior. The dogs had "holed" a groundhog. Tony was standing by enjoying the scenery, the quiet, the breezes and the smell of the woods. Junior was very busy digging out the groundhog. He came upon a very large rock and threw it out onto Tony's foot. Tony thought that Junior would have to carry him off the mountain.

One time Tony and I were playing poker with Junior. We had made all of the bets and counter bets, etc. It was time to show the cards. I had three jacks. Your dad had a pair of queens. He did not see my third Jack. He thought that he had won and was reaching to drag the pot toward him. I looked at him and said "o.k., what else you got?" He looked astonished, jumped up and leaned over to look at my cards and said "You Heffer". I am going to have to get some glasses!" I told him that he could call me a heifer anything as long as I was taking his money.

A little neighborhood boy Jason liked Junior and Irene a lot. . He would come up and sit and talk to them. One day he was over by Alan Jones's house, which was just below Junior's house across the creek, trying to till his garden. He was having trouble tilling the slope there with a front tine tiller.

Junior hollered over and told him to turn the tiller down hill and give it some gas. The tiller took off down the hill with Jason in tow. The tiller pulled him into the creek. Junior said that he woke up in the middle of the night, started thinking about it, and started laughing all over again. The next day, Jason told Junior, "June Cloud, I'll never believe you again."

I was able to go with Junior and Tony a few times on their squirrel hunting, groundhog hunting and ginseng hunting trips. I enjoyed the trips into the mountains immensely. Junior would act like a tour guide, stopping every few yards or so to tell me about some plant or pile of rocks. After awhile, when he could see that I was having no trouble keeping up with them, he took off directly up the hill. I felt like he was testing me to see if this woman could keep up with the men. I never fell behind and this seemed to impress Junior.

One time, when I went hunting with them, the dogs holed a groundhog. I was sitting down slope from the hole where Junior and Tony were trying to dig out their quarry. What they did not know, was that the wily old groundhog had an escape route. The groundhog came out of the alternate hole and ran across my lap. I started yelling, but Tony and Junior could not hear me for the barking of the dogs and kept digging. Some times we didn't catch any animals or find ginseng, but we did not care because we had a wonder full time.

55

Memories of Labor Day Weekend
with Junior and Irene Cloud.
by Tiffany B. Cloud,
daughter of Donnie Cloud

Every Labor Day weekend I venture off to Harlan, Kentucky, a small south-eastern town in the corner of the state. Living there, in the very back of a deep forested holler, are my two grandparents, Tilman and Irene Cloud.

Usually the Friday before the weekend begins; my uncle Roger picks me up and we set back to begin our four-hour journey. Once we arrive I am usually greeted by my two smiling grandparents who I haven't seen in a year and my dad and step mom who come down from Pennsylvania. My granny seems to have gotten wiser at her rip old age of 73 and my grandpa a little funnier at 74.

Saturday mornings are the same every year also. My step mom and I would wake up before the sun did to go with my Papaw Cloud to the flea markets in Tennessee. "All the good stuff will be gone if we wait too long," he says. He insists we go there. "That's where the good ones are," he says. We didn't care it was only over the mountain. This year was no different. My, who hides his money because he trusts his own hands more than he trusts the banks, promised my step mom a quilt this year.

When she found the thirty-five dollar quilt she wanted he had to make sure it was in top condition before he'd let any of his money go. Later on that day he slipped me thirty-five dollars as well. "You will probably win it back from me when we play poker tonight" I said. "Don't use it for that dar-ling," he says in his southern drawl.

Usually I bring a friend down with me to experience real country living. But, this year I decided not to. I figured this would be the last year for my annual trip, with college and all, so I wanted to spend more time with my and granny.

Sunday is the day for my uncle Roger and dad's, (Donnie) yearly golf out-ing. This is a time for them to bond and for me to spend some quality time with my grandparents. So, this year I went shopping all day with my granny. We went to Walmart, the store of all malls down there, and the local pro-duce stand. Then we went out to eat at Wendy's, there my granny shared countless stories of the way it used to be. She recalled to me the days when she was little and she was too poor to buy a hamburger like the one we were eating, so she had to eat pinto beans smashed between two pieces of bread. How my grandpa would hide a pack of cards under the table when he played poker with my dad and uncles so he would always win their money.

My granny has been taking care of him for the last couple of years since he was diagnosed with Leukemia. This year was the first year I could actually see the toll it has taken on him physically. He isn't as strong anymore to take me fishing for minnows in the creek bed or hiking up to the old coalmines. I guess he figured while I was down there he should give me a memento to remember him by. When he handed me the funny wooden hillbilly figurine, I busted out with laughter. He told me the overalls on the man looked just like his and the big bottle sitting next to him was moonshine, just like the stuff my made many years ago. The carved detailed figure reminded me of him, this was definitely something I would never forget

Nothing will ever compare to the warmth I feel when I'm down there. The joy I get from hearing stories about when my papaw slaved for hours in the dark mines, picking coal, or about when my granny worked countless hours to support her four kids will compare to nothing. Labor Day by far is the day I look forward to most all year.

56

In Searching of my Family History

I started getting interested in my ancestors in the mid 1990s. My father had some written family trees that he had received from some cousins and gave them to me.

My Presley cousins were researching their ancestors earlier than when I started. I had heard stories of the people and information that they had discovered.

I talked to them about the things that they had found, when I was in Kenvir visiting my family and they were there from Ohio. On one visit Helen had made copies of some pictures of Presley ancestors and gave them to my mother for me. I was looking at the pictures and came across a lady from the early 1900s who was posing for a photographer.

Chills ran up and down my spine because I was looking at my own image. This lady was named Minnie Hall. She was the sister of my Great grandmother Drucilla Hall Presley. I felt like I was reincarnated from her.

No doubt about it I was hooked. I wanted to find out more information about her, if I didn't find out anything else about my ancestors. She was married to a Turner and had her first child, a son. The person who helped her deliver her son, apparently did not clean out all the afterbirth. She became ill. Her husband took her to one doctor to another trying to get help for Millie. No one would help and she eventually died. Her son grew up hearing how his mother lost her life giving birth to him. When he was an adult he took his own life.

The local Harlan, Kentucky newspaper had been doing a special each year regarding the history of the county. The reporter would interview people in the towns to get their stories before they were lost. My mom saved those papers for almost ten years. She remembered them when I got interested in searching my ancestors and gave them to me one summer while I was visiting her.

When I would visit my family in the 1990 my father and I would sit down and talk about our ancestor Benjamin Franklin Cloud and his brothers. He gave me a handwritten family tree that he received from his cousins from West Virginia. They were the children of his father's sister Ida Cherako.

Most of my stories about the Cloud family are Memories from my father. My mom shared all her Memories of her family. She also shared stories about all the Cloud family that she got to know after she married daddy and moved to Stretchneck holler.

I bought a computer for my daughters got on the internet. They needed the internet for school and later college. I began exploring the internet too. I left inquiries in all the Harlan County web sites I could find.

My first contact was a cousin from Philadelphia. His great grandfather was the brother to my great grandfather. His great grandfather was Alexander Cloud and mine was Benjamin Franklin Cloud. I gave him my address over the objections of my daughters. I was given a lecture about the nuts that were on the internet.

Eugene Cloud sent me quite a bit of information. I received the first family tree from him. I found more people on the internet who gave me information about my Cloud ancestors.

My father's stories led me to the Claiborne County Genealogy Site. I found census records on my Cloud family.

My cousin Helen and her daughter, Kim were still working on their family tree in the late 1990s and early 2000, she began sending me copies of death certificates, legal documents, pictures. Anything that they thought I could use for my research she mailed to me. Unfortunately Helen died last year and she cannot be here to see all the information that I have acquired from more people than I can count, turn into a book.

Helen's daughter Kim has a web site that has a huge amount of information that she has shared with me. I recently received pictures from some Thomas relatives that used to live in Dizney. They discovered my web site and offered the photos to me. I have truly been blessed in my research to have found so many relatives and former friends who used to live in Dizney who knew me and my family.

The following are excerpts from my web site guest book from all the years that I have been working on my web site. Some were lost at one point and I had to rebuild my site.

You can see more pictures and family stories at my web site: www. geocities.com/portiagay

57

Guest Book Entries of Family, Friends and Strangers Who Found My Original and Second Web Page

First Name: Gene C.
Comment: Portia, it's nice to see that you've got a tribute to those hardy and stoic souls of Harlan County. Their stories need to continue.

First Name: Sherry
Comment: Portia what a great job! Can't wait to see Allison's baby's page. I know you will keep us updated and I am looking forward to it. Keep up the good work. Love Ya!

First Name: John and Maryann
Comment: Good to learn about your family. Keep up the good work.

First Name: Alison B
Comment: I am glad that you are finally writing down your stories. They are very interesting. I liked hearing about the tales when Jen and I were younger. You are a very good storyteller. I think that you should make a book and get some money. Love You Mom

First Name: Joan
Comment: Portia—What a great job! I really enjoyed reading about your family and how you grew up. I have always been aware of your creativity but your storytelling is top notch.

First Name: Tony and Debbie
Comment: Surprise! Surprise! We finally made it to the Web! Very, very impressive! We are on Jill's computer across the road. It's a really great job, Sis. We really enjoy it.

First Name: Howard
Comment: I am the brother-in-law of Freeda Halline Presley. She is the daughter of Clark Presley and Sara Emmaline
Presley

First Name: Peggie
Comment: Great Job Portia. Keep up the hard work. Will talk to you soon.

First Name: Tony and Debbie
Comment: We are finally online. After you wake up from fainting, e-mail us!

First Name: Geri
Comment: My name is Geri Delph Fessel. I am the daughter of Etta Lee Delph, granddaughter of Nancy Cloud Pace. Great granddaughter of Benjamin Franklin Cloud and Judith Wynn. I am so glad that I was sent this site. It reminds me of home. Thanks so very much. Geri

First Name: Vilda Leora Presley Woods
Comment: Hey, enjoyed the trip down Memory lane. Although I was born in Louisville, Ky, Momma, Daddy and the rest of the brood could remember more. I am the 10th child of Clyde Greene and Minnie Mae Presley. Will visit again. Leora

First Name: Shawn Cowden
Comment: Great page of Harlan, Ky. I am from London, Ky. Take care.

First Name: Herschel
Comment: Very nicely presented. There are Shoemaker's in my family also from Virginia. Might be cousins also my youngest brother had polio. I know what you went through.

First Name: Jewel

Comment: I am the daughter of Carl Turner from Greasy Creek, Ky, Lil Abner Branch. My mom is a Northerner from Michigan where I was born and raised. My parents were divorced when I was 7 years old, but I remember going to Ky 3 or 4 times when I was little.

First Name: Mark
Comment: Portia I like your web page and enjoyed reading it. Your Mom & Dad make me feel like I am one of their boys when I visit.

First Name: Angie
Comment: Just wanted to say hello. This is a great site.

First Name: James
Comment: Hi, My father was born in Colloway County. His name was Jesse, brothers Raymond, Virgal & Ross. My father was married to Etta Grace Hoskins. She had five brothers and sisters. They lived on the Cherokee strip also.

First Name: Roberta Presley Herron
Comment: Clyde and Minnie Presley's daughter

First Name: Hazel Vanessa Presley Waldrop
Comment: Clyde and Minnie Presley's daughter

First Name: Bobby
Comment: My great great grandparents were Benjamin Franklin and Nancy Middleton Cloud also.
First Name: Sharlene
Comment: Good job I noticed where you recall an Apple Stack Cake that your grandmother used to make. On the above page I have listed a recipe for a stack cake that my grandmother used to make. Please check it out and let me know if it is close to the one your grandmother used to make.

First Name: Ann
Comment: Enjoyed visiting your site. I am a Cloud too, but not your Clouds. I am descended from Jeremiah Cloud.

First Name: Sharon Bodet

Comment: Sara Cloud is my great grandmother, so we are cousins. Sarah is the daughter of Ben Frank and Nancy Middleton Cloud. Sarah married William Cudge Thomas and my grandmother is Pokey Thomas who married Henry Wynn. My Thomas relatives are from Yokums Creek.

First Name: Sheila
Comment: Hey Cuz. What a great job! It brought back so many great Memories and tears to my eyes seeing the old pictures, especially of Mamaw and Papaw. I am proud to be an Appalachian!

First Name: Angeline
Comment: Portia, wonderful job. Oh, the Memories you brought back. Thank you so much

First Name: Kim Dean
Comment: Great job!

First Name: Walter R. Presley
Comment: I enjoyed your piece on your grandpa Presley because my mother's parents, Bleve and Ethyl Eaton met in Harlan County when my grandpa was a miner there. Also, my father was a Presley, as I am.

First Name: Terry Cloud Ber
Comment: Hi Portia! It is so great what you have done. Good for you! I enjoyed it soooo much!

First Name: April
Comment: I enjoyed reading all the information that you have compiled. I too am a descendant of William H. Shoemaker. He is my 3rd great grandfather.

First Name: Trena Caudill
Comment: Your up-bringing was a lot like mine. It was "the good ole days" How can we ever forget!! Thanks for all the interest you have taken. My mother was a Hall from Perry County, Ky. Daughter of James Rant and Leona Hall.

First Name: Danny

Comment: I like your page and I have added your link on mine also. Good Job.

First Name: Barbara Sue
Comment: It was great do more.

First Name: Dee
Comment: You did a great job. I know a lot of your relatives, your Aunt Pauline and mother Irene. I am looking forward to more history of our part of the country.

First Name: Glenda Hamblin
Comment: I live in Kenvir now. My maiden name was Gilbert. I lived in Michigan for thirty years. I'm new on the computer.

First Name: Sharon (Lee) Dibari
Comment: I grew up in Kenvir (Dr. Office and Club House Camp) I was born in 1949. I remember a lot of your family names from school, etc. I too left Kenvir (in '63 when I was 14). We moved to Ohio. I have thoroughly enjoyed reading about your family and your life.

First Name: Danny
Comment: I've been checking out your site. You have a lot of great family pictures. Sure enjoyed looking at them and reading the stories of your family history. I have added a link to your site to the Harlan County Links page.

The above comments were posted on my first web site. I had another 25 to 30 other comments that I had archived, but were lost before I printed them out.

First Name: John
Comment: Loved the website. Does anyone remember John Thompson. Or his Aunt Deltie, member of Locust Grove Baptist Church.

First Name: Lana
Comment: Enjoyed greatly. Wonderful pictures! Your Dizney classmate Lana Soloe Davidson. Thomas, Clay Granddaughter

First Name: Laquita Thomas Spivey
Comment: Loved all I saw on your web-site. What a wonderful place to live at that time in my life. I still think of Dizney as my home place. I still love it.

First Name: Roger
Comment: A real nice website, Portia. Ill send you more pics. Born in a house just a rocks throw up from the mouth of Stretchneck. Schooled and worked there. Would like to live there again. At ease, Rog

First Name: Elaine
Comment: Wonderful photos, wonderful stories. Its good to find a link to my past. Thank you for this great site.
First Name: Corky
Comment: Love the site. Decended from Chockley King/Kissiah Brewer. Surnames in Harlan County are King, Tomlinson, Brewer, Blevins, Witt, Johnson/Johnston

First Name: Stanley
Comment: Really nice to find this page.

First Name: Marlin Ray Wright
Comment: My Cloud line is thru my maternal grandmother, Mary Ella Cloud. Her father was Tilman Howard Cloud, son of John Farmer Cloud, Son of Jeremiah b. 1792, husband of Karon Berry Cloud and son of William Cloud. Jeremiah and family immigrated to Saline Co., Arkansas

First Name: Arli Dick Lay
Comment: I thought the photos were cool. I have you in favorites. I will come back often. When you or anyone else has time come by my home on the web. Drop me a note in the guest book so I will know you were there. Type at you later.

First Name: Lanny (Cuz)
Comment: GREAT

First Name: Rachel
Comment: I think this is wonderful to look back in time at your ancestors. Thank you Portia for all your time in doing this.

Surnames: Presley, Wynn, Middleton

First Name: Linda
Comment: Faye Nell Presley, daughter of Elmer and Maudie Presley says Hello. How are Ya?

First Name: Angela Kinney
Comment: Thanks Portia for all your work on the website. I love the photos and all. Keep up the good work.
Surname: Jones, Blevins, Cloud

First Name: Vickie Fuson
Comments: Great pictures

First Name: Shelly
Comment: Hello Portia. My name is Shelly Blevins Music, my father is Kenny Blevins. I have enjoyed looking at the pictures you have posted. It was great to see my dad. I have heard great things about you all my life. I hope someday to get to meet you.

First Name: Tanya
Comment: Loved reading your family stories. Just started on my husbands Cloud family. His great grandmother is Mania Cloud married to Kennon Harris in Arkansas. Not sure how they fit into yours, but I stumbled upon your site and really enjoyed it.

First Name: Sheila
Comment: As always I enjoy reading about our family. Great job!

First Name: Montford
Comment: Great site. Excellant Pictures. I love and miss the mountains. Harlan connections: Ledford, Farmer, Skidmore

First Name: Ricky
Comments: Portia, I am glad you are rebuilding your site. If I can help I will. Just tell me what you need and I will try to get it to you! I am the son of Ralph Cloud, who is the son of Simon Cloud. Me and my father have the same middle name, which is Frank.

First Name: Kim
Comment: Hi Portia. Glad to see that you have a start to getting your site back up. If there is anything you need, just holler. My site is entitled My Kinfolks of Ky and Beyond.
Surname: Presley, Jones, Brewer, Satterfield, etc.

First Name: Sheila
Comment: Glad to see that you are rebuilding the site. I really miss the other one and read it often. Always enjoy the pictures. Keep up the good work.
Surnames: Grubbs, Pace, Cloud, Presley

First Name: Debbie
Comment: Great job Portia. I have enjoyed looking at your pics, and the stories are wonderful. I remember your house up in the holler. I was there a time or two!
Surnames: Middleton, Singo, Miracle

First Name: Bonnie
Comments: This is one of the very best sites that I ever have visited. What a wonderful history for us from your area. You did a wonder job. Thank you for sharing our history.

978-0-595-46480-7
0-595-46480-7

Printed in the United States
111485LV00004B/138/A